global Christianity

the life we're called to live

Bo Cassell

Nazarene Publishing House
Kansas City, Missouri

Copyright 1999
by Nazarene Publishing House

ISBN 083-411-8246

Printed in the United States of America

Executive Editor: D'Wayne Leatherland
Assistant Editor: Edie MacPherson
Cover Design: Marie Tabler

Unless otherwise indicated, all Scripture quotations are taken from the *Holy Bible, New International Version*® (NIV®). Copyright © 1973, 1978, 1984 by International Bible Society. Used by permission of Zondervan Publishing House. All rights reserved.

Permission to quote from the following copyrighted versions of the Bible is acknowledged with appreciation:

The *Contemporary English Version* (CEV). Copyright © by American Bible Society, 1991, 1992.

The Holy Bible, New Century Version (NCV), copyright © 1987, 1988, 1991 by Word Publishing, Dallas, Texas 75039.

The *Revised Standard Version* (RSV) of the Bible, copyright 1946, 1952, 1971 by the Division of Christian Education of the National Council of the Churches of Christ in the USA.

The Living Bible (TLB), © 1971. Used by permission of Tyndale House Publishers, Inc., Wheaton, IL 60189. All rights reserved.

From *The Message* (TM). Copyright © 1993. Used by permission of NavPress Publishing Group.

Acknowledgments

I am surprised that so often, when authors pen the dedication of their book, the list they include is so short. I have so many people to thank and whom I wish to honor. This book is dedicated, with much gratitude and appreciation, to . . .

My parents, George and Mary Ann, and to my brother, Jordie (who would throttle me unmercifully if I didn't mention him)
   . . . for giving more to me than I have ever asked for.

The Youth in Mission students
   . . . for inspiring me and for living out Global Christianity summer after summer.

My friends
   . . . for inviting me to walk beside you as you walk with God.

My pastors throughout the years—Hal Bonner, Norm Shoemaker, Lyle Pointer, Ron Salsbury, Dave Pendleton, and Dana Preusch—
   . . . for modeling lifestyles that are truly outward focused.

Jon Johnston
   . . . for taking me to China, where I became a global Christian the instant I heard a Chinese girl say, "You are the first Christians I've ever seen." I have never been the same since.

And the three students from my church who will attend NYC '99, for which this book was commissioned: Chad, Peter, and Tiffany
   . . . may this book and the conference impact your life with God's vision so that you, too, will never be the same again.

Contents

Introduction	**7**
Part 1: *A Global Mind-set*	**11**
Chapter 1: What Is a Global Christian?	11
Chapter 2: Are You World-Ready?	19
Part 2: *A Global Vision*	**27**
Chapter 3: Global God	27
Chapter 4: Global Mission	35
Chapter 5: Global Living	43
Part 3: *Becoming a GLOBAL Christian*	**56**
Chapter 6: God-Centered	57
Chapter 7: Learning the World	63
Chapter 8: Outward-Focused	69
Chapter 9: Burdened for the Cause	75
Chapter 10: Available to the Call	81
Chapter 11: Living the Lifestyle of Missions	85
Epilogue: *A Call to Action*	**93**
Endnotes	**95**

Introduction

I am growing dissatisfied with common, ordinary, everyday Christianity. I sense that more and more Christians are likewise no longer content with an ordinary, everyday experience. The run-of-the-mill understanding of what it means to follow God will no longer suffice . . . and rightfully so! Run-of-the-mill Christianity lived out (or, more accurately, *not* lived out) by the average Christian bears no resemblance to the real thing that Jesus Christ describes so clearly in the Bible.

The good news is that we are rightly fed up with this kind of Christianity. The bad news is that we have not replaced the average, mediocre, generic brand of belief with anything different. We continue to progress from average to average—wrestling with insignificant issues in our churches, living small, quietly desperate lives, and never dreaming big dreams for our personal walk with God.

Only the living Christ can rescue us from this trap. The latest fad can't help us. Neither can the new program from the church down the street. Not even learning better methods of evangelism—complete with the latest trinkets from the Christian bookstore—can truly get us out of this rut. Only a real immersion into Christ's blood, only a fresh word of His voice, only His hand brushing the tears from our faces will satisfy our hunger for God.

We must be dissatisfied with the common experience of Christianity if we are going to go on to greater heights. Common Christianity can be full of busyness and activity and yet be completely missing a critical level of energy and passion. Common Christianity can be full of churchgoing but empty of worship. Why is this?

What does this have to do with "global Christianity"? Everything. This is the crucial thesis of this book from this point forward: global Christianity is not common Christianity. Global Christianity is much more than what we often see in our lives, but it is nothing less than all that Jesus called us to when He thought we were worth dying for. Global Christianity is real Christianity.

Have you noticed? We've just begun to talk about Christianity, and already I've had to use three words to describe what we are talking about (common, global, real). This is part of the problem. We've unintentionally created different degrees of following, different "levels" of Christianity—some common and mundane, others exceptional and authentic—and now we're almost required to add a modifier in front of the word so everyone will know just what type of Christianity it is that we're talking about.

When did Christianity become so bland and disinterested in reaching this world that we have to add an adjective in order to describe what we were talking about? We don't say, "Pour me a glass of the wet water." Water doesn't need this modifier. Water is wet.

When did we stumble upon different types of Christianity? When did we begin to allow there to be more than one way to follow Him? When has following Jesus meant anything less than all the way? When did the word *Christian* cease to mean anything less than "little Christ," and when did we let those who call themselves "little Christs" become anything less than just that? Why must we add modifiers— "real Christian," "true believer," "global Christian"? When did Christianity in and of itself cease to mean anything less than all of these?

It was when we started to get water that wasn't wet. It was when we allowed ourselves to settle for living in dryness and accepted a half-lived-out life as the standard, still keeping the title *Christian*. We allowed ourselves to be called "little Christs" even though our living resembled nothing of the life of Christ. It was when Christians allowed dry ones and false ones and unreal ones to pass themselves off as the real thing. It was when we began to accept second best from ourselves and from each other.

Introduction

What we have done is something that Jesus warned us not to do. "If the salt loses its saltiness, how can it be made salty again? It is no longer good for anything, except to be thrown out and trampled" (Matt. 5:13). Again in Revelation Jesus vividly describes His feelings toward a lukewarm, going-through-the-motions faith—a Christianity that is in name only and not lived out fully:

> I know you inside and out, and find little to my liking. You're not cold, you're not hot—far better to be either cold or hot! You're stale. You're stagnant. You make me want to vomit. You brag, "I'm rich, I've got it made, I need nothing from anyone," oblivious that in fact you're a pitiful, blind beggar, threadbare and homeless. . . . The people I love, I call to account—prod and correct and guide so that they'll live at their best. Up on your feet, then! About face! Run after God! *(Rev. 3:15-17, 19, TM).*

It is when Christians stop running after God and begin to casually stroll through life that the problem arises, and it is a problem with global consequences. It is when we become disinterested in the world that the world suffers. When we love only ourselves and cease to love this world as God so loved the world, then we have ceased to be global, and we have ceased to be everything God has called us to be.

This is the point of it all. As long as there are Christians out there who are anything less than "real" or "true" or "global," then the world outside the church will experience the same dissatisfaction with Christianity that we sometimes face within church walls.

The truth is this: to be a Christian means to be real, because we have thrown away the masks we hide behind so that we might see the real, living God face-to-face with no hidden part unexposed. To be Christian means to be global because the living God is the God of the whole earth. If we are to become like Christ, then we are to be on a mission to reach this world just as Christ was, willing to lay down our lives in the process—anything less is unchristian. To be anything less would be like being dry water or flavorless salt or dark, hidden light.

No, we shouldn't have to add *global* to modify the word *Christian*. Every Christian should be a global Christian by his or her very nature. That's what it means to be Christian. It's only because we have lost the vision of what it means to follow the global God that we have to redefine what it means to be truly Christian . . . and thus explain what it means to be a global Christian.

PART 1:
A Global Mind-set

CHAPTER 1

What Is a Global Christian?

Need a quick definition? Global Christians are Christians committed to reaching this world for Christ no matter what the cost. They have seen the world and know the needs, and no matter what job they do, they will for the rest of their lives commit their time, energy, and resources to reaching the world for Christ.

Global Christians are about changing the face of this globe for God. They are about expanding God's kingdom here on earth.[1] They are about making a difference wherever they are, in little ways and big ways, for whatever time they have here on earth.

This has very little to do with going on a mission trip or doing global kinds of things. It is not about venturing out into the globe on a mission trip so that I can feel good about what I have done or so that I can call myself "missions minded." It has *everything* to do with discipleship. It has *everything* to do with surrendering my very self to the Lordship of Christ. *Then* I do missions because I am near to the heart of God—God cares for the world out there, so I must go into it!

Global Christianity is nothing short of living out the words of Jesus, "You are the salt of the earth" (Matt. 5:13). We are to be active and flavorful and useful. We are to be the light that infuses a dark world like beams of sunlight through clouds. Jesus didn't call you to merely be the salt of your neighborhood or the salt of your particular nation. His statement was "You are the salt of the earth." Jesus seemed to have the whole earth in mind when He spoke of our influence and activity as believers.

Some people use the term *world Christian* to describe what we're talking about. The terms are essentially interchangeable. The point of adding either word (*world* or *global*) is simply to remind us of what we lost when we so casually started calling ourselves Christian but quit being like Christ. To be like Christ is to love the world—the whole globe of it—the way God loves it. It means realizing that God has included me in His purpose and plan to bring light to the world. This is nothing different from what it means to be truly Christian. Every Christian should be involved in affecting the world in this way.

David Bryant, author of *In the Gap*, uses the term *world Christian* to explain the kind of person who has taken up his or her role in the "gap." The gap, he explains, is the difference between God's planned purposes for this world and the actual fulfillment of those purposes. He describes the world Christian as one who is standing in this gap, taking seriously God's love for the world, and living out the fulfillment of God's purpose:

> A World Christian isn't better than other Christians. But by God's grace, he has made a discovery so important that life can never be the same again. He has discovered the truth about the Gap, the fact that he is already in it, and the call of Christ to believe, think, plan, and act accordingly. By faith, he has chosen to *stand* in the Gap as a result.

Some World Christians are missionaries who stand in the Gap by physically crossing major human barriers (cultural, political, etc.) to bring the gospel to those who can hear no other way. But every Christian is meant to be a World Christian, whether you physically "go" or "stay at home" to provide the sacrificial love, prayers, training, money, and quality of corporate life that backs the witness of those who "go."

World Christians are day-to-day disciples for whom Christ's global cause has become the integrating, overriding priority . . . for them. Like disciples should, they actively investigate all that their Master's Great Commission means. Then they act on what they learn.[2]

This is exactly what we are talking about when we talk about being a global Christian. It is someone who is totally sold out to God's purpose, being thoroughly convinced there can be no "in-betweenness" of living, only a standing in the gap between God and the lost and a living to bring the two together.

One ordinary man who caught a glimpse of what it means to be a global Christian was Jim Elliot. Jim was a missionary in the 1950s and died on the mission field, killed with spears by the Auca Indians—a people for whom Jim left everything to reach. Even as a youth he had a vision for reaching the world. While in college, Jim took the world seriously, organizing prayer efforts to focus on missions and vigorously challenging his fellow students to address the call of Christ on their lives. Jim Elliot took seriously the claim of Christ upon his own life. He was not the kind of person to casually quote John 3:16, "For God so loved the world . . ." He took the words seriously. He knew that God had called him to do the same.

The Super-Christian Myth

When Jesus said, "You are the salt of the earth," He didn't indicate any subgroupings of believers. He didn't, for instance, split believers into two groups—one group of very committed followers who are to be the salt and a second group who watch the rest go about the business of following. There are not two grades of believers—those who *really* follow and those who *sort of* follow. In truth, the whole point of the story is to say that salt without taste isn't much good! Believers who don't have passion and commitment for following Jesus all the way are no good at all. If the flavor of Christ doesn't exist in your life, what use are you for flavoring this world? In the same way, there's no rank of "second-string believer" or "bench-warming Christian."

Just as there's no category for "half-baked believer," there isn't such a thing as the "super-Christian." There is only Christian. There's no higher rank of achievement where I can strive to outserve you to win the "grade A" stamp of approval. We're all in this together, and we are all called to the same standard—to be like Christ. More specifically, we are called to live like Christ in the world. The Christian norm, the standard of following, is the believer who is committed to living a lifestyle of being like Christ, who has surrendered his or her whole life to His cause, and who has given up personal desires in favor of God's desires.

It's not being a superhuman or super-Christian. Quite the contrary. In fact, this is the *minimum* requirement. When we talk about surrendering everything to reach this globe for Christ, we are really talking about the minimum that is required of us if we are to wear the banner of *Christian*. This level of commitment is expected of *all* believers. Jesus said, "If people want to follow me, they must give up the things they want. They must be willing to give up their lives daily to follow me" (Luke 9:23, NCV). Another translation has Jesus saying, "You must forget about yourself" (CEV). Again He said, anyone "who does not give up everything he has cannot be my disciple" (14:33).

This is an amazing statement! Think about it. Anyone who doesn't give up everything for Jesus cannot be His disciple. *Can't!* Not *may not be able to* or *might be difficult*. Jesus said that there's a cost involved for anyone who would follow and then explains exactly what that cost is. The cost of following is everything. And yet He expects that from *everyone* who follows. Anyone who wants to be a disciple must be willing to give up everything. Discipleship is not for super-Christians only.[3] Discipleship is meant for anyone who professes to follow Jesus. It's the minimum we are called to be.

Is it possible that we have not counted the cost of discipleship? It may be time to test ourselves and see how we stand up.

Face-to-Face with My True Self

This challenge may seem harsh, yet God calls us to examine ourselves, and Jesus asks us to count the cost of following. Sometimes it is hard to be completely honest with God and myself. There's no fooling God; He sees us as we really are. Further, the Bible cautions us not to fool ourselves. What if I look at myself and find that I fall short of what God has called me to be? Yet it's only when I take a close look at myself that I can begin to make a change.

It comes down to a matter of integrity. Have I really been honest with myself? Does the face I wear at church on Sunday match the one I wear the rest of the week? Integrity means that I am the same through and through. Inside and outside. In front of a large crowd or when no one is watching. I don't change based on where I'm at or what I'm doing.

The trouble comes when I don't examine myself with total honesty, to see if my integrity is intact. I must come face-to-face with my true self.

Integrity on a Global Scale

It is this kind of integrity that is necessary to be a global Christian. Otherwise, we will never look closely enough at our Christianity to see that we may have stopped our obedience once we received God's blessings. We won't see the need for a global concern, a global burden, or global living.

Without this extreme integrity, we will keep on living out what we call "the Christian life" yet never be changed into the likeness of Christ—sharing His burdens, His sacrifice, His love for the lost. Without deep integrity, we will continue feasting on the blessings of God, unaffected by the sight of a starving world around us.

More than anything, this book is a call to honesty and integrity before God—a challenge to receive the call of God upon the life of every Christian. That is, the call to "Go into all the world and preach the good news to all creation" (Mark 16:15). This book is a call to honestly surrender *our whole selves* to the cause of reaching this globe for the kingdom of God. That is what it means to be a global Christian.

Personal Reflection

1. If you were to put a modifying word in front of your Christianity, what would it be: _____ **Christianity**

2. Is there a person you would consider a super-Christian? What makes this person like that? Can you think of ways in which they are simply living what Jesus taught?

3. Stop for a moment and consider how much of your language you used today to justify or explain your actions so that no one would think badly of you. Seriously, take a few minutes and intentionally review your day. How might living in the love of God change our need to justify our actions?

4. Make a list of your sins. Write them out on a piece of paper (you can destroy it later). Take a moment to confess each one to God. Now turn the paper side-

What Is a Global Christian?

ways. Look up the following verses, and write them across your list, right over the top of the words. Use these verses: 1 John 1:9; Rom. 8:38-39; Ps. 103:11-12; Heb. 10:17. How does it feel to have done that? Write your feelings as a prayer in a journal.

Group Reflection

1. Go around the group and share one quality you like about your best friend. Discuss whether or not this person would still be your friend if that quality were missing.

2. Now share one quality of being a Christian. Discuss whether or not a person could still be a Christian if those qualities were absent from his or her life.

3. Talk about whether or not we should need to use words like *real* or *active* to describe our Christianity.

4. Have someone read the first two paragraphs of this chapter aloud. Discuss why it is important for all Christians to be committed to reaching this world for God.

Chapter 2

Are You World-Ready?

I remember buying a new operating system for my computer several years ago. It came in a package that was labeled in big letters "WORLD READY." It was the first time I had seen a computer system was capable of functioning in more than one language and writing style. What potential! This new software program made my computer capable of working in Spanish or German or even Chinese and Japanese using Chinese and Japanese characters! I'm not talking about just the capability of writing and printing in these languages, but it made the computer capable of *operating* in them. In other words, someone from Japan could use my computer, and they would be able to operate it without knowing any English. The menus, the programs, the windows—everything would operate and be labeled in Japanese. Now that's what I call being world-ready!

When we speak of being a global Christian, we're talking about being a Christian who is **world-ready.** A global Christian is one who can embrace other cultures because he or she knows that God is the Creator of all. Global Christians are prepared to serve those who are in the world with a loving sensitivity. They don't look in judgment upon the lost just because they don't practice the Christian culture. They don't enter into the world as know-it-alls, but rather as ones who come humbly to serve their world as Christ did. They're into compassion, not competition. They are ready for ministry across the globe in other cultures or across the street in the not-too-distant world of their neighbors and friends.

Jesus was **world-ready.** He left His heavenly home and came to earth as a humble servant. He was Lord of all, yet He took on our culture and lived among us. It's impossible to imagine what He gave up by leaving heaven, but the Bible is clear about how far He was willing to go to reach this globe with His love: all the way—*to death on a cross.* Philippians makes it clear that Christ's attitude was key— "he humbled himself" (2:8). That's our starting point for our attitudes and beliefs. We begin to become world-ready by taking a close look at what we really believe and by putting those beliefs into action.

My View of the World

My view of the world affects my whole life. The way a group of people views life is called a worldview. A worldview is like the glasses through which we see and interpret everything. If the lenses in the glasses are tinted red, then our whole view of the landscape around us will be have a reddish hue. In the same way, if we are taught certain values, these values will carry over and influence our decisions about life.

Another way to put it is to think of a worldview like a map. If my map is hand-drawn, with no good landmarks or directions, then I am likely to get lost. However, if my map is accurate, and drawn by someone who really knows the area, I'll probably have no problem finding my way. It all depends on how closely the map matches the true landscape. A worldview is like that. My beliefs must match the truth.

A worldview is a shared way of seeing life, and it explains how we look at the following areas:
- *what we value*
- *what is most important in life*
- *what we believe*

- *where we came from*
- *our place in this world*
- *what is good and evil, right and wrong*
- *who we are—our identity*
- *how to solve the world's problems*

Our particular worldviews have a tremendous impact on the way we live. Like glasses, however, we look *through* them more than we look *at* them.

Global Glasses

What does your worldview have to do with being a global Christian? Your view of God and this world will change your actions in this world. Unless your "glasses" allow you to see God's plan for the whole world, you won't be motivated to join Him in His mission to reach it. If you don't believe that God is a global God, then you will never want to make a difference in this world for Him. Unless you see the world as lost, you will never be motivated to do anything to reach these lost souls. A global Christian is **world-ready,** and to be world-ready we must have a global worldview.

We must exchange the glasses we have been given by this world and put on glasses that allow us to see the world as God sees it. We must focus our eyes on the needs of this world—needs that break the heart of God—and then see ourselves as God's hands in this world to meet those needs.

When someone becomes a Christian, it changes the way he or she sees things. The same is true when someone decides to be a global Christian. You have to see, think, and act globally. It demands a change and a refocus of your inner values to make room for God's mission to reach this globe.

It's tragic when a person becomes a Christian but doesn't change his or her worldview. A person comes to Jesus, wanting to be good and wanting to be forgiven and wanting to go to heaven but neglecting a change in lifestyle or a change in the way he or she views the world. It's at this point that these people run into problems. They call themselves Christians, but they don't let their beliefs filter into *every* area of their life.

This has the effect of cheapening the grace of God. We attempt to receive all of the blessings He offers without accepting the cost involved in following. Jesus made it very clear that to follow Him involves a cost. Still, many misinterpret the grace of God. They conclude that because salvation is free it is also cheap and that you can accept it without making any changes to your life. This is simply not true. Consider these verses: Luke 14:27; Matt. 5:20; Eph. 4:22-24; Titus 2:11-12; 1 Pet. 2:24; 2 Pet. 3:11. As you listen to the truths of these verses, one truth becomes clear—how we live *does* matter.[4]

Changing Seeing into Doing

To be a global Christian, there must be a joining of faith and life. A global Christian is one who has changed his or her worldview. The new way of seeing things inwardly affects outward behavior.

A person who is world-ready is a person who is ready to lay down his or her life for this world. It is living life the way Jesus lived it—offering oneself as a living sacrifice to God. We give ourselves for God's use, for His pleasure, for His purpose. *What is His purpose?* God's purpose is to reach this world. Global Christians are those who have changed their minds and surrendered their deepest inner desires. They have replaced them with the desire to live sacrificially for God.

Dave, a youth pastor friend of mine, told me of a time when his youth group became world-ready. He had planned the usual kind of mission trip, taking his teens down to the local homeless shelter to serve food. Dave had done his best to prepare them for the event but feared that it was going to be "just another mission trip."

This time, however, the teens caught the vision. Several

of them began to feel that they should be doing something more. They spoke with the director of the facility and told him that they were there to do anything he needed. Their attitude was humble. They came and said, "If you need us to sweep floors—if that will save you money—then we will sweep the floors; if it's cleaning the toilets, then we'll clean your toilets."

The director told them that what he really needed was volunteers who could work with the homeless and teach them how to read. Many of the people who came to this shelter couldn't read or even fill out a job application, so volunteer teachers were a very real need.

At first, this seemed like more than the teens had signed up for. It would take weeks to meet this need, and it would require a deeper commitment than a one-time visit. However, the group decided to do whatever it took to meet the need. At this point Dave, the youth pastor, almost dropped out of the picture—*the students took over!* The youth group raised money to enroll several members in a course where they could be licensed to teach reading for a certificate. They committed to going down to the shelter every Tuesday night to help the people there learn to read and to fill out applications. Parents began to get involved driving their kids back and forth to the homeless shelter.

This youth group became world-ready when they walked in with a humble attitude. They entered the homeless shelter with the same attitude of Christ when He came into this world—willing to lay down their lives for the sake of the cause. They were simply living out their belief that Jesus would do everything He could for these people; therefore, we should do the same.

Persons who are world-ready have simply integrated their faith into their life. A person who is world-ready not only has changed his or her worldview but also has begun living by faith in this world in order to change it.

I think of Scott Chamberlain. He and his wife, Beth, moved into inner-city Los Angeles to start a church for the homeless population there. Scott had a world-ready mind. He knew that the homeless had no worshiping body that they could call their own. So he started one. But Scott knew it wasn't enough to simply start a church on skid row while he, the pastor, drove in and out from a home in the plush, safe suburbs. Scott doesn't just *work* at a church in inner-city L.A.—he *lives* there.

The Book of James speaks very clearly about the integration of faith and action. "In the same way, faith by itself, if it is not accompanied by action, is dead. . . . You see that [Abraham's] faith and his actions were working together, and his faith was made complete by what he did" (2:17, 22). It isn't enough to simply change our thinking; we must change our lives. It does no good be a Global Christian in thinking only. It's only useful if our faith takes us all the way to doing something to make a difference in this world.

Personal Reflection

1. Read Phil. 2:1-11. In what ways was Jesus "world-ready"? What trait in Him do you most need to bring into your life?

2. What kinds of things keep us from putting our faith into action? Why is it so difficult to get an idea from our head to our hands and feet and into life?

3. Sometimes we are hindered from doing something because our lives are overcrowded. List three things that you may have to sacrifice if you were going to live a world-ready lifestyle.

Group Reflection

1. In which of the following areas is your group the strongest: social activities, serving others, or Bible study? What could you do to balance these better?

2. Go around the group and share what areas of our lives we are most likely to compartmentalize. Write them on a large piece of paper or a chalkboard. Then go back around the group and have each person vote for the top two they find most difficult to deal with.

3. Discuss together the role of humility and surrender in becoming world-ready.

Bonus Group Activity

Plan an Offering Outing. Schedule an inexpensive party or night on the town. You might gather at someone's house for fun and games—something that costs you nothing. Go ahead and charge each person $5 or $10 to attend, and give the money to meet a local need or contribute to a global cause. You may wish to discuss and pray as a group regarding some of the ways to give the money away.

PART 2:
A Global Vision

CHAPTER 3

Global God

Global Christianity starts with a proper vision of God. There is no way to be a global Christian without first seeing God as He really is—a global God.

Seeing God as He Really Is

Isaiah received a call to missions when he first glimpsed the truth about God. And so will we. In chapter 6, Isaiah encounters the holy God in a vision. There before him appears a dreamlike picture of the very throne room of God. He sees the Lord "seated on a throne, high and exalted, and the train of his robe filled the temple" (6:1). There are angels present, who are flying around calling out to one another, "Holy, holy, holy is the LORD Almighty; the whole earth is full of his glory" (v. 3).

Isaiah sees God as He really is. For one brief moment, if only through the cloudy, dreamy mist of a vision, God pulls back the curtain of heaven and allows a human being a behind-the-scenes peek at God. Isaiah's vision reveals several lessons about the God we serve:

- **God is high and lifted up.** Bigger than you've ever dreamed. Seated on the throne, a symbol of power and authority to rule and govern. Just the mere train of His robe is so royal that it fills the entire room. God is seen as so great in this vision that no one else can stand in the room to distract from the greatness of the Almighty.
- **God is holy.** The angel creatures in this verse constantly fly around declaring the holiness of God. Of all of the things they could be shouting about God in His presence, they choose to dwell on His unsurpassed holiness. But God isn't simply "holy." The Hebrew method of indicating degrees such as "good, better, best" was through repeating the same word for emphasis. "Holy" isn't just one of many attributes about God. God isn't simply "holier" than the average person. God, Scripture tells us, is *the holiest*, there is none more holy than He.
- **God is a global God.** Right after the angels declare the absolute holiness of God, they remind us that the whole earth is full of God's glory. The glory of God is not simply for the nation of Israel. His glory is not shown only where there are churches, for that would simply be too small a thing for such a great God. The *whole earth* is full of His glory—the glory of God is revealed in the sea and on land and in the air. It is evident in every heart that receives Him, and His love extends even to those who would refuse Him. The glory of God is meant to go to every corner of the earth, until every person has heard of the wonders of God. It is this very point that leads us to examine our global mission and our global living.

The fact that God has a mission to reach the earth must sink into our own hearts first. We must have an encounter with the bigness of God, such that we come face-to-face with the utter size of God and the power of God and the scope of God's love. This will lead us to the question: Have we actively taken up the partnership to reach this world? The glory of God would not have filled the whole earth until it had filled Isaiah personally. It is only after Isaiah's personal vision of God is changed that Isaiah feels compelled to carry the message to the whole earth. So will it be with us. The glory and holiness of God will not fill the whole earth until it has first filled us—*and changed us.* Then we will feel the same compulsion that Isaiah felt to offer ourselves in His service. Then we will be global Christians.

Seeing Myself as I Really Am

When Isaiah sees God as He really is, he realizes that he has no business standing in the presence of such a great and wonderful Being. Isaiah cries out, "I am ruined! For I am a man of unclean lips, and I live among a people of unclean lips, and my eyes have seen the King, the LORD Almighty!" (6:5). In the light of the presence of God, there is no way to hide our sin or our faults in the dark corners of our lives. The holiness of God exposes our sinful shams and our self-deceptions.

There *is* good news, however. In Isaiah's vision, the angel comes with a coal from the altar to touch Isaiah's lips and burn away his sin so that he might stand in the presence of God. But we have something greater than a coal. We have the very blood of Christ, the sinless Son of God, shed for us. The good news is that God will not only forgive us but also make us holy as He is holy. "If we confess our sins, he is faithful and just and will forgive us our sins and purify us from all unrighteousness" (1 John 1:9). Because of Christ, we, as Isaiah, can stand in His presence.

Seeing Life as It Really Is

Isaiah's vision takes us through a process. It begins with drawing near to God. When we draw near to Him we see Him as He really is—high and lifted up. When we see God as He really is, we begin to see ourselves as we really are—in need of His cleansing. When we draw near to Him and are cleansed, then we are able to hear His voice clearly.

When we stand in the presence of God and listen to His voice, we hear what Isaiah heard. He heard the voice of God calling His people to join Him in His mission to reach the world, "Then I heard the voice of the Lord saying, 'Whom shall I send? And who will go for us?' And I said, 'Here am I. Send me!'" (6:8).

God has a mission and a call for us if we will listen to Him. God's mission gives purpose to life. Life as it is really meant to be lived is life filled with meaning and purpose. We are called to share God's love and take His message around the whole globe.

The Point of It All

I want to be clear on this so that there is no confusion. It would be easy to put the cart before the horse here. This point is key: We seek to be global Christians because God is a global God, not because being global-minded is a good thing to do. We don't seek to earn points with God either, as if we could show the Lord our "global merit badge."

As much as this book is about becoming a Christian who is globally oriented, the point of our life here isn't really *missions.* Our fulfillment does not rest solely in missions. It's about God. And God is all about missions.

We don't become global Christians because this is something God wants us to do. We don't change our worldview to see the world the way God sees it merely to feel like we're doing the right thing. We don't "go global" to earn favor with the Father or to feel "more Christian."

We become global Christians in the same way and for the same reason Isaiah did. *We draw near to God.* Life on earth is all about worshiping the Creator who gave us life. God is central. When we draw near to God to love Him, we find that this God is "crazy in love" with this world. We hear His heart's cry, we draw near to Him, we see Him as

He really is . . . and we are changed. We see ourselves as we really are, and God begins to shape and cleanse us.

Blessed to Be a Blessing

God has blessed His Church again and again by doing amazing wonders among people who believe and know Christ. He delivers us from our bondage to sin. He provides for our needs and has given us a place of our own prepared for us in heaven. He has ensured victory in the battle against the powers of evil in this world. More than anything, He has given us His own Son as a demonstration of this love.

It is clear we have been blessed, but we have been blessed in order to share it. Blessed to be a blessing. We have been called by the global God to share His riches with the people of this globe.

In *Catch the Vision 2000*, Bill and Amy Stearns describe God's unchangeable desire to bless His people and our response to this passion:

Think over the energy you are throwing into life right now—trying to be the best you can be, trying to get ahead, to be a better Christian, a better family member, a better *you*. Why work so hard? Why ask so often for God's blessing on your life?

If it's to have a nicer, happier life, that's not a bad goal. . . . But in the here-and-now, biblical discipleship is never described as "nice" or "easy."

God does want to bless you. But not to make your life easy. He'll bless you because He's got a demanding job for you—a specific task, one that lays down rails to guide your major life decisions, to keep you from spinning your wheels in Christian self-improvement. . . . It's more like being born into a family business—everybody is naturally expected to take part in the Father's work.[5]

From His Globalness to Ours

God calls us to holiness by saying, "Be holy, because I am holy" (Lev. 11:45). In the same way, our Christianity should be global because our God is a global God. God's globalness impacts our globalness. Since God loves this whole earth on a global scale, there's no room for selfishness if we are going to follow the global God.

Following a global God impacts our lives at all levels. For example, there is no room for racism in global Christianity. No one can say that his or her race is superior, for we all stand on equal footing before God. A song sung to Jesus in Rev. 5 makes this clear: "You are worthy to take the scroll and to open its seals, because you were slain, and with your blood you purchased men for God from every tribe and language and people and nation" (v. 9). God's heaven is a multiracial, multicultural, multilingual heaven! If we are truly followers of the living God, it will be reflected in our acceptance and love of those who are different from us.

Additionally, our Christianity should affect our use of our resources—our food, money, time . . . anything. God blesses His people in order that they might be a blessing to the world. A Christian lifestyle should reflect this. "Live simply that others may simply live" is a watchword of the Christian life. Christians should lead the way in recycling, food distribution, and giving to the poor. Giving with compassion should overflow from thankful hearts. The normal Christian life should include a global stewardship of possessions. Our lives should reflect God's desire to care for this world.

Our God is such a big God that His rule over the whole earth should shape us completely. We cannot hide ourselves away in isolation, because God is out there weeping with the broken . . . and we should be too. Our God is continually searching the earth looking for the lost, and where He is, there we should be also (John 12:26).

Global Christianity is centered upon God. It's about a big vision of who God is and what He can do through us. God *is* big. He rules this entire universe, calls stars by name, and sets the earth in motion. It's when we draw near to God that we hear His heartbeat. Global Christianity is more about intimacy *with* God than it is about getting out there and trying to do something great *for* God. It starts with, ends with, and is centered upon God. Nothing can motivate us better than close exposure to the deep, deep love of God. We get that exposure by drawing close to the Father in prayer and worship.

Personal Reflection

1. Read Isa. 40. Pick out three phrases that describe how big God is. Write them down and next to them write your prayer of praise to the global God.
2. In what ways do we sometimes miss the point of it all? How do we sometimes put our work for God ahead of God himself?
3. Describe the process by which we move from loving God to loving our neighbor and the world. How does starting with loving God help us love others?

Group Reflection

1. What is one way God has shown himself "as He really is" to you?
2. Share your future dreams. What job would you want to do if you could do anything? Where would you live? Then discuss whether or not some of our dreams

would have to change to fit with God's plan to reach this world.

3. Plan one way you will seek to be a blessing with everything you have been blessed with. Make a list of all the resources God has given to your group. Then make specific plans how you will share the blessings this week in order to reach out to others.

4. Talk about what it means to love God intimately. Share ways we can practice that love. Make a covenant with each other to remind one another to spend a set amount of time with God this week.

Chapter 4

Global Mission

Missions comes from the heart of God. The God who created this earth and everything in it loves His creation dearly. God was willing to go to great lengths to prove this love, even sending His Son to die for this lost world. Jesus describes His mission by saying that "the Son of Man came to seek and to save what was lost" (Luke 19:10).

Jesus examines the heart of God in Luke 15. Here we find three stories, all of which illustrate where our global mission comes from. The last story is the famous story of the lost son, often known as the prodigal son. After many years of wild living, a careless young man returns home, not to the rejection and disgrace that he anticipated, but to the forgiving, outstretched arms of a loving father. The first story tells of a shepherd who loses 1 of his 100 sheep. He leaves the 99 sheep to search for the 1 lost sheep. Jesus explains the meaning of the stories, "I tell you that in the same way there is more rejoicing in heaven over one sinner who repents than over ninety-nine righteous persons who do not need to repent" (Luke 15:7).

The shortest story, sandwiched in the middle, is one more way Jesus communicates the same message about the heart of God: "Or suppose a woman has ten silver coins and loses one. Does she not light a lamp, sweep the house and search carefully until she finds it? And when she finds it, she calls her friends and neighbors together and says, 'Rejoice with me; I have found my lost coin.' In the same way,

I tell you, there is rejoicing in the presence of the angels of God over one sinner who repents" (Luke 15:8-10).

A Sheep, a Coin, a Son

Jesus is making a comparison in each story. In the story of the woman and the coins, God is like the woman, and those who are far from God are the lost coin. Here He gives us a tremendous picture of the missions heart of God—He is turning the lights on, sweeping the house, and "searching carefully" until He finds His lost one. Imagine! God is sweeping the world right now, looking for those who are lost to Him. He won't quit until He finds them.

Jesus compares the lost to a coin. In God's eyes, they are a lost treasure. They are not looked upon in judgment, as if God were searching after them like a policeman tracking down a criminal. Instead they are viewed as valuable. They are worth searching for. They hold such value to God that there is great rejoicing when these souls are found!

The other interesting components in each of these stories are the ones who aren't lost. What about the 99 sheep? The nine coins? The older brother who never left his father? These seem to be compared to the people of God—His "already found" ones, who are safe in His possession, safe in the flock. Yet all three of these stories are making one point: God's *priority* is the lost.

That doesn't mean that God doesn't love His people. Hear the words of the father to the older brother who never left home: "You are always with me, and all I have is yours." These are words of love, acceptance, and belonging. But, as the father explains to his oldest son, he simply had to rejoice because his lost son is home safe again! He does not rejoice to diminish the obedience of the older son. The father is simply overcome with emotion at the return of the son he thought he had lost.

The 99 sheep certainly are of value to the shepherd. The nine coins obviously are worth more at the bank than just one coin. Nevertheless, it is *the status* of that one coin, *the condition* of that one sheep that captures the attention of those concerned. They are lost. It is their lostness that makes them the priority.

God's Priority Is the Lost

God leaves all the found ones to sweep the earth for the lost ones. The lost are His first priority. It should be ours as well. If we are to be God's Church or God's youth group, our priorities should reflect the heart of God. Once we are located safely in the flock or the treasure chest, we cannot afford to become distracted, turning our focus to taking care of the saved ones. Could it be we spend too much time on ourselves, polishing up the found coins and combing the wool of the sheep safe within the pen? There's nothing wrong with improving ourselves, striving to become better servants of the Master, but wouldn't it be even better if we were to take action to join Him in His search?

Picture a church or a youth group focused upon itself, thinking of ways to meet the needs of those who are found. They are the kind of group that is more concerned with scheduling enough social fellowship time among themselves than with spending time out there searching for the lost. If a lost sheep wanders into their pen, they might keep their distance because his or her wool is dirty and not neatly combed like theirs. And if a tarnished coin happened to find its way into their treasure chest, they would cringe to associate with it because it wasn't quite as polished as they appeared to be.

Our Mission: Being a Neighbor

Another passage where Jesus speaks of God's missions heart may surprise you. It is the parable of the Good Samaritan. You know the story. Jesus says the greatest commandments are to love God and love your neighbor. One educated young man speaks up and asks, "Who is my neighbor?" Jesus answers his question with a story. A man is robbed and left for dead. Two types of religious persons—who you would expect to offer assistance—walk by and instead offer excuses. Then, a Samaritan—whose people were looked down upon by good religious people, a "bad guy" you wouldn't expect to offer help—is actually the only one to show any concern. Jesus asks a question: "Which of the three was a neighbor to the man who was robbed?" They of course say it was that evil, half-breed, good-for-nothing Samaritan.

There are two important points to this story. The first is that loving your neighbor has nothing to do with finding out *who my neighbor is* so that I can take care of them and avoid everyone else. This approach attempts to find out the minimum I must do to appease God, satisfying my obligation with the minimum requirement. God will have none of that. The second point is that loving your neighbor means caring for *anyone who has a need.* Jesus said, "Which one do you think proved to be a neighbor to the man who fell to the robbers?" The point is not *finding* your neighbor but *being* a good neighbor. Be the kind of person who cares for others. It doesn't matter whether they live next to you. You may find them along the road. If you do, treat them with the kindness you would use if you found your closest friend or neighbor in the same position. Our mission is to act as a loving neighbor to whoever has a need.

Global Christians simply take this mission seriously. If they hear about a need, whether near or far, they seek to be a neighbor. They know that if the family living next door to them were poor and starving, they would be compelled to help. They simply see no difference between concern for those neighbors and concern for the thousands of children who starve to death daily around the world. In either instance, they are compelled to help in any way they can.

Someone may raise the question, "If there are needs here and needs far away, where should we help?" The answer is both. Help wherever you can, whenever you can.

Worship-Driven Missions

What is your motivation to serve? What would make a person want to follow God on this mission in the first place? Do we do it to impress others or ourselves? Do we do it to impress God?

Our motivation for missions should be simple. It is worship. It is an act of love. What we are talking about here could be called *worship-driven missions.* We worship God and love Him, and because we love Him, we want to be like Him. As we draw near to Him in worship, we begin to hear His heartbeat, and we find He is out sweeping the earth to find the lost. Thus, missions is simply an act of worship. It is loving God by offering our bodies for Him to use. We worship through service. Paul says it best in Rom. 12:1, "Therefore, I urge you, brothers, in view of God's mercy, to offer your bodies as living sacrifices, holy and pleasing to God—this is your spiritual act of worship." Our worship is limited without the mission, and without worship, our service becomes mere duty.

Every moment we live, every action we do, every breath we take can be an act of worship to God. Missions should be incorporated at that level, flowing naturally from our moment-by-moment expression of worship to God. Missions is not an activity to check off of a list; it should be as integral to our spiritual passion for God's heart as our breathing is to our physical well-being.

The Story of Sheep Island

Robertson McQuilkin tells a story of a dream, which captures the urgency and the problem of reaching the lost. It is the story of "Sheep Island." It is a short parable that portrays a desperate situation where there are many lost sheep in need of being saved. This parable examines the responsibility of those who know the way and raises the question about what we really believe—about Jesus, about the lost, about this globe.

In a dream I found myself on an island—Sheep Island. Across the island, sheep were scattered and lost. Soon I learned that a forest fire was sweeping across from the opposite side. It seemed that all were doomed to destruction unless there were some way of escape. Although there were many unofficial maps, I had a copy of the official map and there discovered that indeed there is a bridge to the mainland, a narrow bridge, built, it was said, at incredible cost.

My job, I was told, would be to get the sheep across that bridge. I discovered many shepherds herding the sheep who were found and seeking to corral those who were within easy access to the bridge. But most of the sheep were far off and the shepherds seeking them few. The sheep near the fire knew they were in trouble and were frightened; those at a distance were peacefully grazing, enjoying life.

I noticed two shepherds near the bridge whispering to one another and laughing. I moved near them to hear the cause of joy in such a dismal setting. "Perhaps the chasm is narrow somewhere, and at least the strong sheep have opportunity to save themselves," said one. "Maybe the current is gentle and the stream shallow. Then the courageous, at least, can make it across." The other responded, "That may well be. In fact, wouldn't it be great if this proves to be no island at all? Perhaps it is just a peninsula and great multitudes of sheep are already safe. Surely the owner would have provided some alternative route." And so they relaxed and went about other business.

In my mind I began to ponder their theories: Why would the owner have gone to such great expense to build a bridge, especially since it is a narrow bridge, and many of the sheep refuse to cross it even when they find it? In fact, if there is a better way by which many will be saved more easily, building the bridge is a terrible blunder. And if this isn't an island, after all, what is to keep the fire

Global Mission

from sweeping right across into the mainland and destroying everything? As I pondered these things I heard a quiet voice behind me saying, "There is a better reason than the logic of it, my friend. Logic alone could lead you either way. Look at your map."

There on the map, by the bridge, I saw a quotation from the first undershepherd, Peter. "For neither is there salvation in any other for there is no other way from the island to the mainland whereby a sheep may be saved." And then I discerned, carved on the old rugged bridge itself, "I am the bridge. No sheep escapes to safety but by me."[6]

McQuilkin goes on to cite general statistics about the state of our world. Nine out of 10 in this world are lost and apart from God. Three out of every 4 have never heard the gospel of Jesus and wouldn't know how to get off the island if they wanted to. One out of every 2 cannot hear the gospel because there is no one near them in their language group who could tell them. The question is, *What are we going to do about it?*

Personal Reflection

1. What kinds of barriers keep you from standing in the gap between God's mission and the fulfillment of that mission? Fear? Total surrender? What would it take for you to stand in that Gap?

2. Take out a journal or some blank paper and record your reactions and feelings to this statement: "God's *priority* is the lost."

3. Have you recently been inspired in worship to some action? What was it? What was special about that moment of worship that motivated you?

4. How did you feel reading the story of "Sheep Island"? If you were to put yourself in the story, where do you see yourself, and what do you see yourself doing?

Group Reflection

1. Read the parable of the good Samaritan (Luke 10:25-37). In the story, which of the following characters do you identify with the most?
   a. **the Victim** (sometimes feel beaten up and left by the roadside)
   b. **the Priest or Levite** (sometimes have walked by on the other side when I should have helped)
   c. **the Samaritan** (sometimes stop to help others whether I feel like it or not)
   d. **the Innkeeper** (sometimes people dump their problems on me)
   e. **the Donkey** (sometimes feel like I have to support my friends or that they weigh me down)

2. What could be done in your church or youth group to make it more worship-centered and active in missions? What kind of commitment would it take from each individual?

3. Go around the circle and have each one share how he or she will be a good neighbor to the group. Make a commitment to something practical—one or two small ways you will love the other members of the group. Write each one on a paper, and post the ideas as reminders.

Chapter 5

Global Living

Global living is not something you do as a part of your life. It cannot be accomplished as one of several activities to be checked off a list of achievements. Global living is a lifestyle. Global living flows out of a life of worship, a life totally dedicated to God. It comes from taking seriously the claims of the Bible upon our lives and the call of Christ to love the world as He did. The lifestyle of global living demands that we follow the lifestyle of sacrifice that Jesus lived out during His time here on earth.

Our Model for Global Living

The problem is that Jesus is a difficult model to follow. His commitment and sacrifice can only be described as total. He calls us to follow Him, saying we must "carry our cross." In other words, Jesus expects us to be willing to give up everything for Him, including our lives—just like He gave up His life. Jesus calls us to follow Him, but guess where He goes? To the Cross, to lay down His life for the world.

He warns us that this lifestyle is so extreme that we might need to count the cost first. What is the cost? Jesus is very clear on this point. The cost is everything. Jesus paid no less, and He calls us to follow Him without any reserve in our commitment. So, consider the cost. Are you prepared to give up everything for Him? Global living will demand that kind of sacrificial commitment.

A Life of Obedience

As I seek God first and obey Him, global living falls into place. Because God is a global God, when I obey Him I will be living out His will for my life globally. As I listen to His voice, I hear Him call me to get involved in this world.

A lifestyle of obedience begins with a sensitive ear to the voice of God. The Bible says, "Today, if you hear his voice, do not harden your hearts" (Heb. 3:7-8) It was this passage that led me and a group of my college friends to drastically examine our lives and make some pretty critical decisions.

A group of us were talking one day about what God was doing in our lives. Nancy shared this verse from Hebrews and said that she was going to work on listening to God more and on being more sensitive to His Spirit. She saw that as a way to start obeying Him in every situation. "I can listen closely to God, but obedience comes down to my response," she explained. "I still have the choice when I hear His voice—to obey and live what He says, or to harden my heart. It's scary to think of all the little ways I have resisted God and hardened my heart to Him when I should have obeyed."

Several of us were personally challenged that day. We decided that we would commit to obeying that verse—listening for His voice and, when we heard it, not "hardening our hearts," but responding with obedience instead.

I experienced more spiritual growth that year than in any previous year . . . and in almost any year since. I found that I had been resisting God often. Until I started working on obeying God every moment, I never realized how much I had been resisting Him.

You know the feeling. You're there in church and you get that uncomfortable feeling in your stomach and you know that God is talking to you. Maybe the pastor has given an invitation to pray and you feel all nervous, knowing that you should go forward and take time to pray with God. Your mind starts filling with excuses. You'll wait and pray

Global Living

at home because you can take more time there and *really* pray. You're a leader in the church and what would people think if they saw you down at the altar? It might affect your leadership. They might misunderstand and think that something is really wrong.

My friends and I agreed that we were no longer going to live like that. If we heard His voice, we were going to obey. We all started obeying in small ways, and it led to obedience in big ways. That year, my friend Nancy gave up her summer vacation for a two-month mission trip to Scotland. It was that year that God clarified a call to missions in my life. My devotional times with God came alive. I spent two months reading the same chapter in the Bible (1 John 3), and I got something new out of it *every day*. I began to get hungry to actually live God's Word more and more. I began to stop friends in the hallway to ask how they were doing—how they were *really* doing. Living on the surface, with a "Hi how are you, I'm fine thanks" relationship was no longer good enough. I wanted to know what was really going on in their lives so I could pray for them. But it all started with one verse from Hebrews. It all started with seeking God first and learning to obey.

Living for Yourself or for Others

Global living is a series of choices. It starts with the choice whether or not to seek God first—am I going to live for God or myself? Once I put God first, I heard His voice calling me to give my life away for others. He leads me through the greatest command ("Love God with all your heart") to the second greatest ("Love your neighbor as yourself"). We must do both—love God *and* love those around us. Global living is a natural extension of this process. It is simply taking these commands and living them out on a global scale. This may seem impossible or complex, but it's really quite simple, a two-part approach to our lives.

First, we live our lives for others *around the globe*. This means we give our three primary resources—our prayer, our time, and our money—directly to people in need far away around the world. If I know of a need in a world area and believe that through God I can make a difference, then I should do something about it! I don't go about wildly without planning or strategy, but I prayerfully seek the heart of God to direct me to those areas where I can give of my resources.

In 1998 a group of Kansas City residents heard that the government in Guatemala had cut funding to orphanages. News reports came in that children were being put out of orphanages and left to fend for themselves simply because there was insufficient money to keep the orphanages in operation. This group of residents committed their time and money to go to Guatemala to run a house that would care for these orphans. Several of the residents stayed in Guatemala for months at a time to make sure things were being taken care of properly. This wasn't even a Christian group! It was just a bunch of caring people who heard about a need and decided to do something about it. Maybe they weren't Christian, but they certainly understood global living!

Second, we live globally by *making a difference locally*. I can have an effect on this world by living out global principles in my own home and by caring for my neighbors and the world right where I live (my community and town).

An Example from John Wesley

John Wesley lived in the 1700s and started the Methodist Church. Perhaps more important, Wesley modeled a global lifestyle by the choices he made to put God first and others before himself. The following example illustrates how Wesley practiced this global living through the way he viewed his financial resources. This example is paraphrased from an account in "What Wesley Practiced and Preached About Money":[7]

On one cold, winter day, John Wesley went out and bought some pictures for his room. At the time he was

Global Living

teaching at Oxford University and enjoyed a good salary, much more than what he was used to growing up. He returned home to hang his pictures up when one of the chambermaids came to his door. Wesley noticed she had no coat or anything else to protect her from the cold except for the simple linen dress she wore. Wesley searched his pockets for some money to give her to buy a coat, but he found he did not have enough left. God began to convict his heart, reminding him that the money he had earlier used to purchase pictures for his room would more than have covered the cost of a coat for this woman. Wesley examined himself and asked himself, "Will your Master say, 'Well done, good and faithful steward?' You have adorned your walls with the money which might have screened this poor creature from the cold! O justice! O mercy! Are not these pictures the blood of this poor maid?"

This incident changed Wesley's lifestyle in terms of his use of money. Back in the 1700s, Wesley earned 30 pounds (the British equivalent of a dollar) in the first year after this encounter. He found he could live off of a mere 28 pounds, so he gave away the other 2. The next year his income doubled to 60 pounds, but instead of increasing his style of living and spending more on himself, Wesley continued to live on 28 pounds and gave away the remaining 32. The next year, he earned 90 pounds and gave away 62. The year after, he earned 120 pounds, giving away 92 pounds to the poor. At one point in his life he earned over 1,400 pounds (making him a very wealthy man in that day!), but still Wesley lived on the bare minimum and gave away the rest.

Wesley's motto toward money was *"Earn all you can, save all you can, so that you can give all you can."* His attitude was world-focused. He didn't satisfy himself with the minimum requirement ("God asks me to give a 10 percent tithe to the church, so that's all I'll give"). Instead, he viewed his finances from a lifestyle approach—*all* of his money was God's.[8]

The Life of No Regrets

We can talk all we want about global Christianity and about the mission of God and about how we all should get involved, but it ultimately makes no difference until we get down to real life. The truth is, there can be no global Christianity without global living. And there will be no global living without Christians who are willing to make the necessary sacrifices.

If we are serious about this issue, then we need to consider the cost of committing to this cause. Likewise, what is the price of a half-hearted commitment? Or of not committing at all?

The cost of a life uncommitted or half-committed can be measured in regrets. When you get to the end of your life, what will you regret the most? Successful businesspeople have concluded that no one on his or her deathbed looks back and wishes to have spent more time at the office. Instead, he or she looks back and regrets not spending enough time with family. What might a Christian who lived life halfway look back and regret?

Luke 18 tells a story about a wealthy young man who comes to Jesus and asks what he should do to have eternal life. Jesus tells him what every good Jew should already know, that he should keep the commandments and so on. The young man isn't satisfied with this answer, however, and reports that he has done this ever since he was a little kid.

Jesus then challenges the rich young man at the core of the real issue: "You still lack one thing. Sell everything you have and give to the poor, and you will have treasure in heaven. Then come, follow me" (v. 22). The very next line tells us that the young man became very sad, because he was very rich. Jesus had challenged him to give his life away and live for others, and we find the young man goes away disheartened because he wanted to keep his wealth for himself.

I wonder what happened to this young man. I wonder

Global Living

how the story ended for him. When he got to the end of his life, did he look back on the day he came face-to-face with Jesus? Did he have any regrets? Did he ever ask himself the question, "How would my life have been different if I *had* totally given everything to God that day?" Did he ever wonder, "What kind of life did Jesus have in store for me when He asked me to give everything I had to the poor?" Did he ever stand on the balcony of his expensive house in his royal robe, with his coffers full of gold and silver, looking over all of his land and property and livestock, and quietly wonder to himself, "Was it worth it?"

Bill Borden was heir to the Borden dairy fortune. To inherit millions, all he had to do was step in and take over his father's business. But young Bill received the call of God upon his life. He felt like God was calling him to Africa. To his family's dismay, Bill packed up and left for Africa. His father was angry that he would sacrifice the family business and leave everything for a foreign land.

Within two weeks of his arrival, Bill contracted meningitis and died shortly thereafter. His family was furious when they received the news. It was such a waste, they thought, to lose their son to such foolish dreams. As they were shipped back from Africa, Bill's possessions were unpacked one by one by Bill's father. There among them, he found Bill's Bible. Opening it, he saw an inscription dated shortly before Bill's death, just about the time Bill was enduring the greatest suffering of his sickness. It read simply, "No reserve. No retreat. No regrets."

This young man understood that following Christ meant total sacrifice and surrender. Obedience to God may mean we have to give up something, but God has something greater in store. C. T. Studd, missionary to China, understood this. His slogan was, "If Jesus Christ be God and died for me, then no sacrifice can be too great for me to make for Him." Jim Elliot left everything to serve as a missionary to the Auca people in Ecuador and was murdered by them. Before his death by spear on a riverbank, he wrote,

"He is no fool who gives what he cannot keep to gain what he cannot lose."[9] All of these men knew what it meant to live a global lifestyle. They all knew the meaning of "no regrets."

A Life Lived for the Kingdom

This life lived with no regrets is a life lived for the Kingdom. This is part of choosing whether to live for yourself or for others. You can live your life all the way but choose to live it all the way for yourself. When you look back on your life, what will you have done for eternity? What will you have done to make a difference in this world? Or in someone else's life?

Back in the 1980s, Steve Jobs, cofounder of Apple Computer, knew he had to get a new president for his company. If Apple was going to go anywhere, Jobs would need to get a good business person to run things. He made an appointment with John Scully, then president of Pepsi-Cola. Jobs sat down face-to-face with the chief officer of this multinational corporation, looked across the desk at the talented executive, and said, "John, are you going to make sugar water for the rest of your life, or are you going to come with me and change the world?" With that, John Scully left Pepsi to head up Apple Computer.

I meet many Christians with great plans. I talk with many who have the design of their life all figured out. They are going to go make a million dollars and settle down at a nice quiet church where they can attend the potluck dinner once a month. And I sometimes want to tell them (and sometimes I do) that their plans are just sugar water! When are they going to give up all *their* plans so that God has room to do what *He* wants to do? What are they doing for the Kingdom? What are they doing for eternity? The plans to grow up and get married and get a job and make lots of money and have a house are all very nice plans. But where does the kingdom of God factor into this equation? Where is

Global Living

the sacrifice and surrender that is evident in the lives of the people God uses?

When you look back on your life several decades down the road, would you trade all of those things (the house, the money, the quiet life in the suburbs) for one chance—just one chance—to make a difference in someone else's life? Would you trade all your plans and dreams for one opportunity to be used by God to change the world?

A Wartime Lifestyle

Most young people today have limited knowledge of the participation and sacrifice it took to win World War II. They may remember the Persian Gulf War and understand war to be something that takes place in 100 days or fewer. It may be inconceivable to youth today to think that a war can actually last for four years or more. In that kind of long-term battle, the war is fought not only by the soldiers on the front but also by ordinary people behind the lines. The use of resources to support the fight was crucial in World War II, and so it is in our battle to reach this world.

The truth is, we are at war. We are in a battle to reclaim the earth, to set free the prisoners of war who were lost and captured by the king of darkness. Our mission is the fulfillment of the verse, "The kingdom of the world has become the kingdom of our Lord and of his Christ" (Rev. 11:15). We are in a battle with the powers of darkness to reach the souls of the lost. If we are at war, we need to live a wartime lifestyle.

In the early 1940s during World War II, every citizen was expected to contribute to the war effort. The war was not just something fought in some faraway land. It was fought in the everyday lives of every citizen. In the United States, gasoline was rationed so that fuel could be conserved for the military. People were asked to collect scrap metal, rubber tires, all to be recycled for the war effort. Their lives revolved around making the war effort a success. After all, if they failed, what would happen? The world would have fallen to evil.

One dramatic contrast occurred on the luxury liner *Queen Mary*. This big boat, second in fame only to the *Titanic*, sits in retirement in the harbor in Long Beach, California. Now a museum piece, the *Queen Mary* shows how the wartime lifestyle affected every part of life, even that of this once-famous cruise ship. During the war, the *Queen Mary* was enlisted as a troop transport and was converted for that purpose. Once the giant ship permanently docked, the striking contrast could be seen. As a display, one side of the main dining room was restored to its prewar condition. Tables were covered with fine linen; pure silver knives, three different silver forks, and an array of silver spoons were arranged meticulously; and no less than 15 plates and saucers completed the luxurious place settings. The other side of the room showed the wartime setup. Instead of 15 plates, there was 1 metal tray with indentations where the food was put. There was one fork, period. The boat's sleeping compartments were also on display, with bunk beds stacked eight high to the ceiling, explaining how they were able to convert the normal passenger capacity from 3,000 to 15,000 during the war. It must have frustrated the boat's original designers, but it had to be done. The survival of the country depended on it.[10]

The apostle Paul understood the realities of a sacrificial lifestyle. He said, "I do not account my life of any value nor as precious to myself, if only I may accomplish my course and the ministry which I received from the Lord Jesus, to testify to the gospel of the grace of God" (Acts 20:24, RSV). He did not count his own life as of any value compared to the battle he was fighting for God. Like a good soldier, he was willing to give up everything for the cause, including his life. And he did.

Sometimes it takes going on a mission trip or getting outside of your culture to realize that there are more resources in North America than in much of the world. For many North

Global Living

American Christians, half of the battle is learning what Jesus meant when He said, "From everyone who has been given much, much will be demanded; and from the one who has been entrusted with much, much more will be asked" (Luke 12:48). What if those in the United States during World War II had not adopted a wartime lifestyle? What if those who had the resources back in North America had kept them to themselves while those on the battlefields of France or Germany went without food and fuel? From those who had more, more was asked. Should it not be the same for us in our spiritual battle to reach the world? We are called to adopt a wartime lifestyle. As Paul said to the Corinthians, "Now it is required that those who have been given a trust must prove faithful" (1 Cor. 4:2). We have been given the trust of using our resources for God's kingdom's sake.

And so the lost sheep continue to wander about lost, without food, being taken away by evil wolves, and with no one to lead them to safety. Day by day more sheep are lost as casualties of the goings on around them. Meanwhile whole groups of shepherds eat well and live full and blessed lives. They sit at home in their warm surroundings, venturing out only once or twice a week for the shepherds' meeting, where they talk about tending the sheep. "My sheep wandered through the mountains and hills and over the face of the earth, and there was no one to search for them or care about them. . . . As I live, says the Lord God, you abandoned my flock, leaving them to be attacked and destroyed, and you were no real shepherds at all, for you didn't search for them. You fed yourselves and let them starve . . . Therefore the Lord God says: I will surely judge between these fat shepherds and their scrawny sheep. . . . And I will notice which is plump and which is thin, and why!" (Ezekiel 34:6, 8, 20, 22b, TLB).

There is only one thing more frightening than being unaware that there's a war going on around you: knowing that there is a war, a cause to fight for, and not caring enough to change your lifestyle to bring about the victory.

Personal Reflection

1. What is the difference between *doing missions* and really living a global lifestyle?
2. What kinds of temptations are there to keep us from living globally? What keeps us from living a holy life?
3. Read 1 John 2:15-17. Which of these areas do you struggle with the most?
4. When you look back on your life even right now, is there anything you regret? Why or why not?
5. How drastically would your life need to change for you to adopt a wartime lifestyle? List at least five specific things that you could do to live a life closer to a wartime commitment.

Group Reflection

1. Divide the group into two or three smaller groups. Have each group make a list of everything Jesus gave up to do His mission. See which group can come up with the most.
2. Next, try to make a list of everything our culture says we "need" and every possession we purchase for convenience. Try to figure out which ones we really do need to survive—the absolute necessities.
3. Discuss together which has the most benefits—the normal lifestyle or the wartime lifestyle. What traps and complications are added to our lives when we don't live sacrificially?

Global Living

4. Go around the group and share your answers: *For me to live globally, I would need to _____*

_____

_____.

PART 3:
Becoming a GLOBAL Christian

In this section, we will examine some practical ways to begin living out our global Christianity. We will focus on several aspects of global Christian living, looking at specific examples that we can apply in our day-to-day lives. You've already been introduced to the basic principles reflected here in the previous two sections. Chapters 6 through 11 will examine these issues in greater depth.

For easy identification, we will be using the GLOBAL acrostic to organize the next six chapters. Each chapter will correspond to one of the letters in this acrostic and will represent one of the primary ingredients to being a global Christian. These guiding principles are:

a global Christian is . . .	**G = God-Centered**
a global Christian is committed to . . .	**L = Learning the World**
a global Christian is . . .	**O = Outward-Focused**
a global Christian is . . .	**B = Burdened for the Cause**
a global Christian is . . .	**A = Available to the Call**
a global Christian is committed to . . .	**L = Living the Lifestyle of Missions**

CHAPTER 6

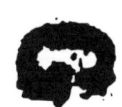

God-Centered

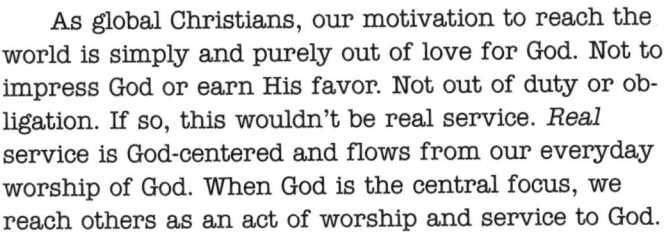

As global Christians, our motivation to reach the world is simply and purely out of love for God. Not to impress God or earn His favor. Not out of duty or obligation. If so, this wouldn't be real service. *Real* service is God-centered and flows from our everyday worship of God. When God is the central focus, we reach others as an act of worship and service to God.

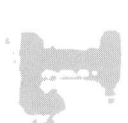

Because we do it to honor God, we are concerned with *how* we reach out (our method) and *how well* we reach out (our effectiveness). We will seek to *love* people into the Kingdom, because we understand that God loves them, and we want to serve them as an act of serving God. Reaching the world, or serving others, isn't just a job or a task—it's an act of worship. The focus then is upon God—not upon us and our work or even upon those we seek to serve. God is central.

With God as our focus, we then have our purpose, our power, and our plan for outreach. The purpose is to honor God and worship Him through service. The power comes from the joy of knowing Him and from the presence of the Holy Spirit in our lives as we draw close and love Him. The plan comes to us as we spend time listening in prayer.

A Life Centered on Spending Time with God

Centering our lives upon God comes from daily spending time with Him in the reading of His Word (the Bible) and in prayer. There's no shortcut here. If we want to live the global Christian life, we must be God-centered. If we want to be God-centered, then we must spend time with Him.

Jesus modeled this kind of God-centered living. Jesus didn't reach the world with just a nice smile and some good stories. Jesus reached the world through a life that was centered upon God. In fact, every time Jesus faced an important moment in His ministry, He faced it from the strength of His prayer lifestyle.

We see this in Luke 6 as Jesus prays all night before He calls His disciples. We see it again on the night before Jesus goes to the Cross (Luke 22). At perhaps the most crucial point in His ministry here on earth, what do we find Jesus doing? Praying earnestly. Practicing His habit of being with the Father.

No basketball player would expect to show up for an NBA basketball game without the appropriate preparation. No real athlete competes without practice. You don't eat doughnuts, watch TV all day, never touch a basketball, and expect to show up on game day and perform like Michael Jordan. To play like Michael Jordan you must practice like Michael Jordan. To do what Jesus would do in any given situation, you must live the lifestyle of Jesus—daily spending time in personal worship of the Father. Sometimes we try to fool ourselves, believing, *If I wear Michael Jordan's shoes, I will play basketball like Michael Jordan.* I will play like Michael Jordan only if I practice like Michael Jordan and dedicate myself to a lifestyle of practice. Daily drills. Extensive conditioning. Only then dare I show my face on the court. Likewise, I will live the global Christian life only if I practice it daily by spending time with the global God.

Ever wonder why students have mountaintop experiences at summer camp or during a retreat, only to come crashing down to the valley when they return home? It's simple. At camps there are times and activities intentionally set aside for sharing about God, daily worship and devotions. Often, none of these things exist when they return home. To keep from going up and down a spiritual roller coaster, these kids should commit to practicing the presence of God in daily personal worship and devotions when they get home. Otherwise they are doomed to continue the up-and-down cycle.

Centering Our Lives

The most important step in becoming a global Christian is sitting at the feet of the global God. To make a difference in this world, we begin by making a difference in ourselves. Spending time with God will make that difference. To change the world, we must first change ourselves. Becoming God-centered is the first step.

What are some practical ways we can live a God-centered life every day? Here are some suggestions.

- ***Settle the devotional issue.***

Decide right now that you are going to make spending time with God a priority. The best way to get to know the heart of the global God is to daily spend time with Him. Time set aside as an appointment with God is often called devotions or quiet time. Being God-centered means making your quiet times a priority.

Determine that you will not struggle with fitting God into your day but that instead you will put God first and struggle to find time to fit everything else in. There's only one way to cultivate this close relationship with God, and it's through a lifestyle of consistent daily prayer.

- ***Start with a commitment to daily prayer and Bible study.***

Begin your journey by setting a daily appointment with God. Feel free to start small, maybe 20 to 30 minutes a day at first. Spend about 10 minutes reading the Bible and reflecting on what you have read. Then take about 10 to 20 minutes just to talk with God. If you're just beginning this practice, you'll probably find that your mind will wander at first. You may even have a tendency to fall asleep. Don't feel guilty. Just center your thoughts and heart back on God.

You can also make this easier by finding an out-of-the-way place to pray. If you consistently go to the same place, your body and mind will get used to praying in that spot, and it will become quicker and easier to settle into prayer as time goes on.

Actually the length of time you spend is not as important as is developing a level of consistency. Make it a daily commitment. Choose a time in the day when you won't get distracted or when others won't be demanding your time. Find a time when you can be alone with God. And stick to it!

- **Practice personal worship.**

Most people define *worship* as a one-hour church service on Sunday mornings. That's not the way a global Christian sees it, though. For a global Christian, worship is a moment-by-moment, everyday experience.

Begin to practice this by making your devotional time a period of daily personal worship with God. Seek to grow in God daily by worshiping Him every time you meet with Him. Consider introducing music to your personal worship times—maybe you'll want to sing a favorite worship chorus or hymn as you quiet yourself before the Lord. Get a journal and begin writing daily "sermons" to yourself based on the scripture you read that day. In your prayers, seek to worship God in moments of silence, listening for His voice, and reading written prayers from devotional writers or the Psalms.

- **Try praying a little at a time, all day long.**

Ideally, devotions done in the morning set the tone for the day. But where schedule and fatigue cripple the spirit, you can still spend time with God at length by breaking up this time throughout the day. This has the effect of remind-

God-Centered

ing you of God all day long. Try this plan of spending 10 minutes in serious prayer, at 6 times during the day. Set a watch alarm for 3-hour intervals at 6 a.m., 9 A.M., 12 noon, 3 P.M., 6 P.M., and bedtime. It may be hard to find an hour block, but most anyone can find 10 minutes if you can make a commitment to focus these times on intentional prayer.

- **Find accountability in others.**

Tell several respectable people in your church about your commitment to spending time with God. Ask them to check up on you weekly to see how you are doing. As much as anything, this accountability will help you achieve consistency. The encouragement and support from these people will provide courage and strength to remain consistent when it might have been difficult on your own.

- **Incorporate service as an act of personal worship.**

Seek out ways to serve others as a way to worship God. Actively look for things you can do for others at least once a week. Most churches could provide a long list of service opportunities. Make doing kind things for people an act of worship. Look for ways to serve others, both those who are believers and those who aren't.

Personal Reflection

1. Is it difficult or easy to make prayer a priority? Why or why not?
2. What keeps us from putting God first?
3. Reflect on the suggested action steps for the God-centered life. Pick one to begin working on this week. Write out your commitment to work on it, and share it with someone who will keep you accountable.

Group Reflection

1. Discuss as a group ways in which you can help one another stay God-centered. Make a list of things you can do to encourage each other. Vote on one thing that each person will do this week to keep everyone God-centered. Plan to report back next week how things went.

2. Brainstorm as a group several ways that you can serve together to express your worship toward God. Select one, and plan on doing some small act of service after your next meeting.

3. Study Heb. 11. Talk about how faith was key to the lives of those listed there. In what ways did faith keep them centered upon God in difficult circumstances? Discuss the role of faith in a God-centered life.

CHAPTER 7

Learning the World

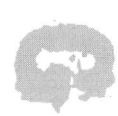

A global Christian is someone who is committed to reaching this whole globe for Christ no matter what the cost. Global Christians have seen the world and know the needs, and no matter what job they do, they will for the rest of their lives commit their time, energy, and resources to the cause of building God's kingdom. To be able to reach the world, you must know the world. Part of accomplishing God's mission is to be aware of what needs to be done.

A global Christian is one who is continually learning the changing world he or she lives in, keeping aware and up-to-date on what's happening in the world. The goal isn't to fill our brains with mere trivia and head knowledge. The purpose is to understand the times so that we will *know what to do* (1 Chron. 12:32). Knowledge is the forerunner to action. Better knowledge leads to more strategic action. If we are going to make a difference in this world, we must understand the state of the world and be aware of its needs.

Christian missions used to be thought of in terms of "countries." But the world has changed. Now we think in terms of "people groups," of which there may be hundreds within one country, speaking different languages and dialects and requiring cross-cultural missions to reach them. We used to talk

about "converting the heathen"; now we talk in terms of training national pastors to handle the task of reaching their own groups. We used to think of sending missionaries only *from* North America; now there are missionaries going out from countries all over the world—including some who are being commissioned to reach the lost in North America itself. The world is changing.

People groups are multiplying. Multiculturalism is flourishing. People are moving away from rural societies into cities, causing tremendous urban growth. The least evangelized part of the world now lies within a span stretching from North Africa, across China and India. It's an area known as the 10/40 Window, because it lies between the 10th and 40th parallels on the map. It is also the most populated area in the world. In the next half century, the world's five largest cities are predicted to be Shanghai (42.1 million), Mexico City (41.5 million), Beijing (36.9 million), Bombay (35 million), and Calcutta (34.4 million). Four of these five cities lie within the 10/40 window and are presently considered to be non-Christian.[11] There's much work to be done, but the Church must learn the world, create strategies, and commit to doing what is necessary to reach these lost urban centers.

Learning the World

To learn the world we must first *gain awareness* through continual study of its places, peoples, and politics. We learn how to pray and where to get involved by becoming aware of the status of global situations, geography, and needs.

Second, to learn the world we must *practice cultural sensitivity* in the nearby world where we live. There are people different from you nearby, no matter where you live. There are people of different races and cultures, of different popularity, of different economic levels, and so forth. Part of learning to love the whole globe as God loves it is learning to love those around us who are different from us.

Learning the World

The following practical ways to learn the world explore both ways to gain awareness and ways to practice cultural sensitivity.

- **Get the world in front of you.**

Get a world map and pin it up in your room. Make sure it reflects as many of the recent changes as possible. When you hear of things happening around the world, locate them on the map. Learn the names and locations of various places. Here's a quick quiz to get you started:

a. *Where is Burkina Faso?*
b. *What countries border Israel?*
c. *Find four Australian cities.*
d. *Which is closer to China—New Delhi or Bombay?*
e. *What is the capital of Uruguay?*
f. *What are the Canadian provinces?*
g. *Croatia is bordered by what other nations?*

Answering these questions doesn't make you an expert, but it's a start! There is plenty to learn about our world. Get an atlas with statistical information (or check one out at the library) and examine the cities of the globe. What is currently the most populous city in the world? Where do North American cities rank in terms of size? Which countries have the most resources? Learn the world by learning where things are in it.

- **Keep up with the news.**

Read the newspaper. I'm not talking about the comics or the sports section. Read the World News section. This may seem like a boring task, but it will provide the global Christian with an instant prayer list. "The Bible tells us what God wants to do in the world; the newspaper tells us where He wants to do it and where we need to be involved with our prayers."[12] Absorb as much information about the world as you can. Consider ways you can take action and be prayerful.

- **Don't be overwhelmed—focus on one area.**

Sometimes learning the world can get overwhelming.

You can take in as much general information as possible, but it also helps to go in-depth in just a few places. Start small. Pick out one city to study and pray for. Learn as much as you can about it and the culture and life there. Focus on that one city or country and begin to get as in-depth as possible. Search the Internet for information. When you check the weather for your own city, find out what's predicted for your adopted city as well. Start listening for news reports of things happening there. Get even more personal through writing letters and E-mail to other students in that city or country. Check with your school about exchange programs. If there are international students at your school or nearby, make their home city your focus of study. Ask them questions about their home.

- **Get out into the world.**

The best way to make a global Christian is to get a Christian out into the world. Participating in short-term mission trips is one of the best ways to learn the world. The exposure to another place becomes lasting because it has been personal. When you have seen a place and can associate faces and memories with dots on a map, you no longer see the world with indifference.

- **Turn from patriotism to appreciation.**

People from the United States are particularly guilty of this. We are very proud of our country, but we don't often stop to think that someone else might be proud of his or her own as well, as different as it may be from North American culture.

Our office once sent a team of college students from the United States to minister in Montreal. We prepared them as we would any other international team, communicating everything they would need to know about crossing international borders and entering different cultures. None of our international teams had any problems . . . except for those traveling into Canada. They violated every rule we told them and were typical "loud Americans." They almost didn't make it into the country! One of our Canadian contacts had to plead with customs and immigration just to allow the team to cross the border. Our team had gone in with the attitude, "It's just Canada," not realizing that they were still crossing into a foreign country with its own patriotism, customs, and ways of doing things.

I'm not saying that we shouldn't be proud of our own national heritage, wherever we're from. We just don't need to flaunt it! Global Christians lay aside their own national pride that they may stop and listen and appreciate other nations and cultures.

- ***Practice sensitivity in language.***

Our words can sometimes wound people. Learn to watch what you say when in another culture or around people who are different from you. Our words can sometimes betray us, and we accidentally put people down instead of building them up. Be careful of words or phrases that might convey any sort of racial or ethnic stereotype. Use caution when expressing generalizations. Don't label individuals or groups undeservedly. What we say and how we say it is important—don't let this be a pitfall for your witness.

- ***Learn a new language.***

English is the first language of only 9 percent of the world's population. Don't assume that those of other cultures will or should speak English to you. People are honored when you attempt to speak to them in their language.

Personal Reflection

1. Think of someone you know who is very different from you. This week, get with this person and ask about his or her world.

2. Learn three new phrases in another language from someone this week. Go back to this person a week

later and practice the phrases. What was the reaction when you tried your phrases?
3. Pick a country to begin to study and pray for. Collect some information from the library or the Internet, and meet with one other person to pray for that place.

Group Reflection

1. Challenge your group to host a party for international students in your community. Make them the guest(s) of honor, and let them know that you are glad that they came to your country.
2. Meet together as a group, and go through your normal routine but allow no English to be spoken during your meeting. When the meeting is over, talk about what it must be like to be a visitor to a place where you don't know the language. How could you be more sensitive to potential visitors from other cultures?
3. Share together what you are going to do to make the world your hobby this week. Quiz each other on what you have learned.

Chapter 8

Outward-Focused

Global Christians are outward-focused. Their lives are about loving their neighbors—a world full of neighbors—by putting God and others first. *Compassion* is an important word to describe the kind of love we are talking about here. Compassion is loving with an outward focus. It's when your needs are more important than my own. I am loving compassionately when you mean more to me than I mean to myself.

I once received a birthday card from a very close friend. The card coincidentally bore the lines from 1 Cor. 13. I've never forgotten what my friend wrote inside. She wished me a happy birthday and then referenced my birthday (May 18). Then she wrote, "This day has been more important to me than my own birthday." I can't tell you what that meant to me, that someone would consider my birthday more important than her own. I felt humbled, and I knew that in her own words, she was telling me she loved me.

Compassionate love is the love of Christ. Jesus came to this tiny globe to love you by giving His life away for you. He died upon a cross to pay the penalty for your sins. Because He loved you, He died in your place. He went through suffering and death simply because you meant more to Him than His own life meant to Him. That's what love is. That is the compassionate kind of love. He came to be with us and sit with us and listen to us—and even to suffer with us.

Loving Globally

To love globally, we simply take our compassion to the next step. As I am learning the world, I see the needs that are out there, and I simply must do something. I am compelled by the love of Christ to get involved in areas of the world that have need or have never heard about God. I begin to follow the example of Jesus and offer my life as a gift of compassion. I obey the command of God to love those near me. But as my love becomes outward-focused, it is continually spreading farther and farther out. It is like the command of Jesus to the disciples, "You will be my witnesses in Jerusalem, and in all Judea and Samaria, and to the ends of the earth" (Acts 1:8). The disciples' commission as Jesus' witnesses started small and nearby, but the ultimate focus was outward, to people farther and farther away (and more and more different from themselves). The final goal Jesus identified was global—the ends of the earth.

Becoming Outward-Focused

Turning our eyes off of ourselves is not an easy task. Below are some practical ways to begin the process. First we begin to put others first, then we turn our attention to the world around us. Our journey toward becoming outward-focused follows the same pattern of the disciples—we start nearby, then move outward to the rest of the world.

- ***Start by loving yourself (and by being loved).***

It becomes easier to focus on others when I know that I'm loved and accepted. Jesus said, "Love your neighbor as yourself," which implies that I must first love myself. Perhaps the best way to begin this process is by getting in touch with how much God loves me. If I can believe that the Creator of this universe and this beautiful world actually loves me dearly, it becomes easier to love myself. God's love makes me valuable. I am not loved by Him because I'm valuable—I'm valuable because I am loved by Him. Reflect on the following verses and consider the love God has for you: Psalms 139:13-14; 100:3; 1 John 3:1; 4:19.

Rest in the knowledge that you are loved by God. Then you can freely give love away because you are not fixed on your own need to be loved. When we are full of God's love, that love overflows to those around us.

- ***Put your family first.***

A global focus doesn't mean neglecting those relationships closest to us (our own personal "Jerusalems" from Acts 1:8). In fact, your family can be a starting point for developing your outward focus. Family is a place where I can learn to put others' needs ahead of my own. Practice patience in your family. Don't get into petty arguments when conflict arises. Learn when to give up your own desires for the desires of others. Serve your family by obeying your parents and going out of your way to do something kind for your family members. Learn to listen to them.

- ***Practice crossing over into other groups.***

Practice crossing over into groups of people and circles of friends with whom you normally don't spend time. It will be awkward at first, and you won't know what to say, but watch and listen for common ground to talk about. Find out what they like and what is important to them. Practice a lifestyle of reaching out to others. Be a bridge person between Christ and a group of people at your school or in your neighborhood. Find those who might not make a connection to Christ without someone to bridge the gap.

- ***Love the unlovable.***

Go to those who are rejected by others. Throw out your claim to popularity. Make friends with a "nerd"; don't be afraid to have lunch with someone from "the wrong side of town." Don't flinch at the smell of a homeless person—give the person a hug anyway. How did Jesus treat the lepers, the diseased, and the outcasts of His day? Certainly not by avoiding them and waiting for someone else to minister to them. He reached out to them and loved them. If we are truly going to be the hands and feet of Jesus, we cannot be selective about who we serve.

- **Take care of the needy.**

There are many ways you can make a difference by volunteering your time and skills—whether or not you have money to give. Get involved with a local homeless shelter or community relief organization. Keep your eyes open for needs in your church and your community that you and your friends could meet. You might volunteer free baby-sitting for a single parent in your church or neighborhood so the parent can go out for dinner or even begin night classes. You might tutor children whose parents both work, helping them with homework while their parents rest.

Personal Reflection

1. Why is it difficult to love others when you don't feel loved yourself?

2. Describe the difference between a compassionate love and a "self-centered" love.

3. How can I keep from just giving a token act of service (just to make myself feel good)? What approach can I take when helping others that will allow me to truly serve them and not just serve them as a way of serving myself?

Group Reflection

1. What is the difference between loving yourself in a good way and loving yourself in a bad (selfish) way?

2. What is one purposeful act of kindness you can do as

a group? Talk about the most compassionate way to carry out that kindness.

3. Have each person think of two people he or she wants to focus on this week and some action steps that could be taken. Have each person write these names and goals on an index card and seal it in an envelope. Collect the envelopes, explaining to the group that the envelopes will be distributed at next week's meeting so each person can check his or her own progress in this area.

CHAPTER 9

Burdened for the Cause

It may be difficult for this generation to understand what it means to be burdened for the cause. Many of us today have grown up in a world changing so fast that we have become detached from it. We are used to being surrounded by the apathy of our peers—people who sometimes don't even care about themselves, let alone reaching out to others.

There's a different way to live life, and it's the way a global Christian lives. The global Christian life is marked by a burden for the cause to reach this globe for Christ. It's a life full of passion and purpose, a life full of emotion and tears, meaning and joy.

What Is the Burden?

The word *burden* is used because those who feel it describe it as a weight upon their hearts, something so strongly impressed upon them that they could not go on with their normal, everyday living without dealing with it. It is a passion for reaching the lost, a hunger to see God's mission fulfilled. It is this kind of burden that brings people to leave everything to go to the lost. It is this burden that brings people to their knees to pray. It is this burden that changes the world.

Catching the Burden

How do we get a burden like that? Simply by seeing the need face-to-face. This is the benefit of the short-term missions experience. People and their needs become real, no longer just some lesson in a book.

We also catch the burden when we accept our responsibility to reach the lost of our generation. Nobody else can do it; it's up to us. When we realize this, we begin to feel the weight of the task upon our shoulders and the urgency of the need. It must be that personal. If we don't take personal responsibility, we probably won't feel the burden and we're likely to do nothing.

Perhaps the best way to catch the burden of reaching the lost is by praying. Nothing can replace standing in the presence of God and catching *His* passion for the lost. Connecting with God's heart in prayer will lead us to action. As we align our will with His will, we are moved to actively participate with Him in those plans.

In the Book of Revelation, the prayers of the saints are described as bowls of incense (a fragrant smoke) rising up before God (5:8). At one point, all of heaven waits for the prayers of the saints to go up before God—and it is only after they do that God springs to action, pouring down fire upon the earth (8:1-5). What power there is in prayer! We must use it!

Becoming Burdened for the Cause

The burden for the cause brings us to our knees to pray for the nations. As we pray, God hears and answers, and He changes us. He begins to shape us into global believers, carrying the burden for the lost. Below are several suggestions for becoming a believer who is burdened for the cause.

- ***Pray for the nations.***

Pray systematically for the nations and peoples of the world. There are a number of ways to do this, and many resources available to help you. There are prayer cards available at most Christian bookstores that list countries and prayer needs. You can also get a prayer map, which is a map of the world listing specific areas to pray for. You could do the same thing with an ordinary map of the world. Spread the map out during your prayer time and pray for the nations one country at a time. Pray specifically for those peoples in the 10/40 Window, stretching from North Africa, through the Middle East, and into Southeast Asia. This most populated area of the world also contains the greatest number of Hindus, Muslims, and Buddhists in the world.

One invaluable resource worth mentioning is the book *Operation World: The Day-by-Day Guide to Praying for the World*, by Patrick Johnstone. It lists all the countries in the world, with specific days to pray for them. It also contains information on that country, about its religions and peoples, as well as a list of basic prayer needs. This book is available at most Christian bookstores.

- **Pray with passion.**

Pray believing that this is a life-or-death matter for the lost of this world. Pray for the cause of reaching this world for Christ. Lay hold of the world country by country, people by people, and don't let go until your prayers are answered.

- **Seal the burden in a commitment.**

Make a commitment to the Lord that you will pray regularly for the nations and that you will give yourself to join God in sharing the burden with Him. Write out your commitment, and keep it somewhere you can refer to it often. You might use the following words to guide you:

Disciple's Pledge[13]

By the grace of God and for His glory, I commit my entire life to obeying Christ's Great Commission. Having committed myself to this world-focused way of life, I will:

1. *Pray earnestly each day for God's work of world evangelization.*

2. Give sacrificially for this cause.
3. Consistently share my faith with non-Christians.
4. Seek to influence others to become global Christians.
5. Go anywhere and do anything God desires.

Signature: _____ **Date:** _____

- **Put your money where your mouth is.**

The Bible says, "Where your treasure is, there your heart will be also" (Luke 12:34). Put your money where your prayers are by giving money on a regular basis to the cause of reaching this world. You may not have much to give, but that's not the point. Give *something*, and let God use it. Practice sacrificial giving, the kind of giving that flows from your passion to be a part of what God is doing throughout the world.

Personal Reflection

1. Which inspires you more: Statistics and information about a need, or someone sharing about his or her work with passion? Why do you choose that one?

2. Is your greatest obstacle to praying for the nations a lack of information or a lack of desire? What can you do about it?

3. If you feel so led, copy down the *Disciple's Pledge* above. Make two copies, and sign them both. Keep one for yourself, and give one to a responsible adult in your church. Ask him or her to post it at home and pray for you and your commitment.

Burdened for the Cause

Group Reflection

1. Discuss with the group: If a burden is like a fire inside your heart, what outside factors have the ability to pour water on this fire?

2. Have each person share a way you can "keep the fire burning" in your group.

3. Try to arrange for a guest missionary speaker to come to your group and share his or her burden for the people he or she served. Ask where the passion to go get involved came from.

CHAPTER 10

Available to the Call

Recognizing and obeying the voice of God is crucial to global Christianity. God is at work in this world, and we are called to join Him in this mission. God calls all of us to serve Him in this way. Further, God places a special or unique call upon the lives of some of His people, asking them to lead His people or to go into the world to serve in particular ways. So there are two kinds of calls—the call upon the life of every believer, and the specific call that God directs to some of us.

The Call to All

All believers have the call of God upon their lives. We are all called to follow in the steps of Jesus, to be like Him, and to act as His agents in the world. Every believer is called to be holy. There are no exceptions. We are called to love God and love one another. We are called to go and make disciples of all nations, according to the Great Commission. This call is to all of us, regardless of our talents and gifts and interests. It doesn't matter what your gift is or how good you are at it. What matters is what you did with it for the Kingdom's sake.

We are all called to invest our lives for God and for His kingdom's sake. It doesn't matter whether

you have the gifts of a pastor, the abilities of a world-class athlete, the skills of a musician, or the talents of an accountant. The question is: How are you using those gifts for His kingdom?

The Specific Call

God does place a specific call upon the lives of some of His children. Don't hear me wrong. This isn't some special badge of honor awarded from on high. Neither does this make those who receive this specific call any more special than those who don't. This simply means that God calls some out for a unique purpose, often to make them His servants in the role of pastors and priests. Just as He called out one tribe of Israel to serve Him as priests, God still calls people to specific tasks or roles of leadership (Eph. 4:11-12). But the fact that God calls some to these specific ministries doesn't cancel the call on all of us to be involved in God's global cause.

Availability = Obedience

To a global Christian, availability means listening and saying yes to whatever God asks, being obedient and responsive to the needs of this world. A global Christian not only learns the world but also is obedient to responding to the facts learned, realizing that a part of fulfilling his or her own call involves a personal response to those needs.

God has called His people to respond to the condition of this world. It is our responsibility to take our role in the world seriously. What are you going to do about the lost? What will you do about the starving? You may not be able to change the world, but it is very possible you could change the world for one other person. The key is to listen and obey. God will guide you and help you. "For the eyes of the LORD range throughout the earth to strengthen those whose hearts are fully committed to him" (2 Chron. 16:9).

Becoming Available to the Call

Whether or not we feel called to a specific ministry, we are all called to obedience and to accepting a role in bringing the kingdom of God to this world. God has called us to be His ambassadors here on this earth. He asks us to be available and respond to His call to global Christianity. Here are some basic ideas how to start.

- **Get involved in some kind of ministry.**

The best way to learn if you are called to something is by doing it. Taking up a ministry and trying it out will help you learn where you fit in God's plan. Get involved helping to teach a Sunday School class at your church. Start a small-group Bible study. Join the choir. Help out in the nursery or assist with clean-up. Talk with your youth pastor or other youth worker about these and other options.

- **Practice listening and obedience.**

Learn to say yes to God in everything, both small things and big. Life would be so much easier if we always said yes to God. So often, Christians have their own plans and their own ideas of what they should be doing, and they just charge right into them, pausing only to ask God to bless their efforts. This is the opposite of being available to the call and really has very little to do with obedience. Learn to listen for God's voice and His direction.

- **Talk with a mentor about your call.**

Spend some time with a responsible elder and discuss the call God has placed upon your life. Find someone who will support you and encourage you in your journey. Make certain it is someone who models the Christian life with integrity and authenticity. Share what you are feeling about being called to live the global Christian life. If you feel a specific call, talk about it with them.

- **Ask the right question.**

Have you ever heard anyone ask, "What is God's will for my life?" I think this is the wrong question. I'd suggest simply asking, "What is God's will?" Don't begin your obedience from your perspective. Start from the place of total submission to God. "Once I know God's will, then I can adjust my life to Him. . . . The focus needs to be on God, not my life!" First we submit to God, then "we watch to see what God is doing around us and join Him."[14]

Personal Reflection

1. Have you ever felt a specific call to ministry? Write out how you experienced it in a journal so that you'll have a record to look back upon.

2. Are there any areas of your life where you struggle with obedience? What about listening?

3. What is the relationship between surrender and ministry?

Group Reflection

1. What does it mean to be available? Discuss how that is different from being committed. Which comes first?

2. Provided the group is comfortable enough with each other, have each person share one thing that he or she struggles with that hinders the ability to listen to God.

3. Ask for volunteers from the group to talk about their own call. Discuss how the call to be a global Christian fits with each individual specific call to a ministry.

CHAPTER 11

Living the Lifestyle of Missions

To live a lifestyle of missions simply means that God's mission becomes your life. You don't just *do* missions, you *are* missions. Missions begins to flow out of everything in your life. Your lifestyle is centered around living for God and for His kingdom. You are focused on loving others. You give your life away in service and in love.

The missions lifestyle is a lifestyle of sacrifice. You cannot live for others without giving up things you would otherwise choose for yourself. Jesus said, "No one can serve two masters" (Matt. 6:24). As we cannot serve both God and money, neither can we serve both others and self. We will have to give up things to follow God and love others the way God calls us to.

What we do with our time, energy, and money does matter. We live on a globe in a "global village" with limited resources. It matters how we use them. It matters whether or not I waste goods, how much I contribute to pollution, and whether my money goes to rent videos or to humanitarian relief. As the Bible says, "None of us lives to himself alone" (Rom. 14:7).

The Nonessentials of Life

It may be difficult to think of giving things up for God. But if we take a closer look, we find that what we give up was probably never really needed at all. Most of our possessions are really nonessentials—things we "need" purely for convenience or entertainment, but items that we don't really need to survive.

Roberta Winter, one-time missionary to some of the poorest regions of Guatemala, relates the story of her embarrassment when her family arrived at their missions post for the first time. They had brought along what had seemed to them to be so little. Yet as their barrels of possessions and necessities—even a washing machine!—were unloaded, the people stared. They couldn't believe someone could own all of that stuff. Winter felt defensive when one young man asked how much the mattress cost. She knew he would not earn enough money in a month to buy one.

Winter continues, describing her family's return to the United States after five years of living with the poor in Guatemala. She explained the feelings of walking into a drugstore for the first time after returning. There were shelves filled with stuffed animals, lined with discount jewelry, and overflowing with toys. She remembers her husband remarking, "There is not one thing here I would take home even if they gave it to me."[15] They had learned to live a missions lifestyle while on the mission field, and their old lifestyle now seemed extravagant and excessive.

From her experience, Winter formulated several principles to guide our lifestyle of missions[16]:

1. **"Our lifestyle must please the Lord, yet it should not in small matters be so shockingly different from those among whom we walk as to make unintelligible the message we wish to convey."** In other words, we must live a life of sacrifice, but if we sold everything and lived on the street, people in our culture might not understand. At that point, our sacrifice would distract from our message.

2. **"A simple lifestyle in the U.S. can still seem extravagant to most people in the world. Yet our geographic isolation does not reduce our obligation in God's eyes to people at a distance."** The point is not to attempt to live at the level of the poorest of the poor within our own culture. We will not be able to do it. Neither is the point to help the poor by raising them up closer to our standard of living. The point is to live sacrificially in order to give away our resources to meet real needs and to care for the poor by assisting with their basic needs for a healthy, safe, and adequately fed life.

3. **"We don't really need most of the things our culture would push off on us. Once we learn to resist social pressure, it is far easier to determine what we really want or need."** As Winter puts it, "We never hesitated to buy something which would simplify our lives, giving us more time to spend on more important things. But *we* determined what we wanted. *We*, not television ads nor social pressure, decided what would help us" (italics added).

4. **"There ought not be any connection between what is earned and what needs to be spent. You don't buy things just because you have the money."** Like John Wesley, we can limit our lifestyle and give away what we really do not need. This one practice alone could change the face of the globe.

A global Christian is called to live simply so that others may simply live. We are charged to live a lifestyle that will make a difference in this world. The key principle behind this is simplicity. Live a simple, sacrificial life. Where do we get the strength to live this way? There is a power in saying yes to God that makes it easier to say no to everything else. John Wesley called it a "new affection"—as he fell deeper in love with God, his love for the things of the world diminished.

Living the Lifestyle of Missions

Here are some ways to simplify your life and begin to live a lifestyle of missions. Remember that we are talking about living a *lifestyle*. Sacrificial living is meant to be integrated into every area of our global Christian life. Sacrificial living is one part of a larger whole. Checking items off a list won't mean you have arrived. These are only a beginning toward an ongoing lifestyle—where everything in my life fits with my overall mission to love God and serve others.

- **Learn to save, no matter how much you earn.**

Practice Wesley's principle to *earn* all you can and *save* all you can so that you can *give* all you can.

- **Live by needs, not wants.**

Don't let your own desires or your culture or the media determine what you need. Understand the difference between needs and wants. Evaluate—is there a better way your money could be used?

- **Push yourself.**

Practice *sacrificial* giving. King David once said, "I will not offer a sacrifice that costs me nothing" (1 Chron. 21:24, paraphrase). Don't just give out of your excess; what does it mean to give away something that you probably won't even miss? Give deeply from the heart, with such generosity that it requires a sacrifice on your part. Remember that giving is not about how much you give but about how much you keep.

- **Make people a time priority.**

Consider your time an investment in people. Don't waste time when you can invest it. As the saying goes, "You cannot kill time without injuring eternity." Purposefully spend time with nonbelievers to make friends with them. You don't have to forcefully witness, just let Christ in you rub off on them. Don't see people as an interruption. Treat others with dignity and honor them.

- **Sponsor a child.**

You can have a direct impact by giving your money to help the poor through child sponsorship. Often these programs provide not just food for the malnourished but clothing and schooling for those who would otherwise have none. If you are interested in sponsoring a child, you can do so through Nazarene Compassionate Ministries Child Sponsorship, 6401 The Paseo, Kansas City, MO 64131.

- **Choose to go against the norm.**

Don't let society dictate how you use your resources. Refuse to spend extra money for designer clothes. Don't jump in on fads or make purchases without thinking. Refuse to let your position or popularity keep you from humble service to those who may be rejected by certain social circles. Stand out from the crowd the way light stands out from darkness.

- **Eat out less.**

Restaurant and fast-food dining is expensive, quickly devouring your extra money. Take the time to pack a lunch. Purposefully set aside the money you would have spent on fast-food into an "offering piggy bank" or a place where you can save up money to give to the poor. You might decide to invite your friends over to your house instead of going out to eat together. Serve them a meal and collect an offering of the money you would have spent at a restaurant. Give that money away to feed the hungry.

- **Empty yourself and walk in freedom.**

I learned this principle from those who minister among the homeless. If you walk for any length of time among the homeless, someone will ask you for money. Some of the workers there choose to carry no money with them when out on the streets. That way they are free to minister without being used. They can build better relationships because that's all they have to offer.

This principle is true in many ways. The more you sacrifice, the more doors it will open for you in ministry. If you are empty of riches, then you have nothing to offer but yourself. Francis was a monk who gave up all his possessions for his ministry. He explained his voluntary poverty this way: "The dedicated man might go anywhere among any kind of men, even the worst kind of men, so long as there was nothing with which they could hold him."[17] If you empty yourself as Christ emptied himself, then you will be able to offer yourself to the empty and broken around you, just as Christ gave himself for this broken world.

Personal Reflection

1. On a piece of paper, list everything you threw away this week. Also list everything you bought. List how many times you ate out. Add up the prices for all the things you spent money on. Next to each item, indicate whether or not it represented a need or a want. For those items thrown away, list whether you could have used them better before throwing them away.

2. On a separate piece of paper, list some ideas of other ways you could have used the money you spent on wants this week. Write out some ways you could conserve resources more efficiently.

3. Keep a log of your time for the next week. Write out on a chart how you spent your days for a whole week. At the end of the week, write out everything you would like to do for God but don't have time for. Insert those goals into your schedule in the places where you're able to identify "time wasters."

Group Reflection

1. Think of ways we could live a lifestyle of missions. From these ideas, formulate a Lifestyle Covenant. Make it a short statement that describes what this

lifestyle is. Then discuss what it would take to commit to that statement as a group.

2. Share what would be the hardest thing to give up for God. Talk about why that would be so difficult.

3. Brainstorm together ideas for sacrificial living that you could practice as a group. Talk about community-based ways to conserve resources, as well as sacrificial offerings you could take. Think about what you could do as a group to volunteer your time for service.

Epilogue

A Call to Action

This book is a call to honesty. It's a call to honesty with ourselves and with the Word of God. It is also a call to action. It's a book designed to force you to examine your life and to make changes to live a life that is more global, more centered upon God and His mission. When you put this book down, I want you to take with you more than a vague idea about "being global." As important as they are, I want to challenge you with something more than honesty and integrity. I want to impart to you *urgency*.

While I was in college in California, a large fire blanketed many of the surrounding Santa Monica mountains in which my school was nestled. I was responsible for one dorm on campus and had the opportunity to direct my dorm residents to evacuate the building for safety. We sent everyone down to the cafeteria, which was away from the mountains and the fire.

I remember going back to my dorm as the fire began to enter the valley where our school was. I quickly went throughout the dorm and calmly directed the residents to the cafeteria, closing all the fire doors as I had been trained.

Then I went back to my room. It was strangely quiet, and the dorm was nearly empty. I put one quick call in to my mother. Then I stood there in silence and looked about the room. I had the gift of a minute to answer for myself, "What would you take with you if there was a fire?"

I looked about my small dorm room. I grabbed my backpack and put my Bible in it. Then I grabbed some books and notes that I needed to study for a test the next day. That was all. I picked up the phone to make one more call, but the lines were already dead. I shut my door and left.

As I left the dorm, the scene was chaotic. There were security officers along the roads telling people to hurry. Cars were backed up at the exit to campus, as panicked students tried to drive away. One girl ran past me, struggling to carry two hastily packed suitcases. A shirt sleeve hung out of one, dragging on the ground. People were running around, and there was lots of screaming.

I looked up. There were flames 5 stories high, covering the mountains around our school. Some of these flames literally shot 40 to 50 feet in the air. There were helicopters flying past now, tracking the fire through its mountain course. One student stopped to take pictures (I saw them later, and they were spectacular). I began to walk to the cafeteria, safe along the road, instructing some that we were headed to the cafeteria. There I met up with some friends, and we passed the time until we were allowed back to the dorms. The fire spread quickly and intensely, but fortunately burned itself out before reaching the buildings or causing any significant damage.

Why do I tag this story on the end of my book? Because it's a lost sheep story. Because it's a symbol of our lives here. The truth is, if you knew there was a fire on its way, you would most likely take action. You wouldn't stop to write a little chorus about fires. You probably wouldn't take the time to debate the theology of fires. You would move. You would mobilize.[18] You might stop for a moment and take stock of your own life, looking around and taking with you only what was an absolute necessity. But then you would move. You would act. You would walk, or even run. You would direct others to safety.

My hope for you is that this book has served as an opportunity to stop and take stock of your life before mobilizing yourself for action. It's time to get actively involved in reaching this globe for God.

Look around you, friends . . . the world is on fire.

Endnotes

1. To be a global Christian means simply to be a Christian the way Jesus meant us to be Christian. Consider this: In the Lord's Prayer, Christ states, "Your kingdom come, your will be done on earth as it is in heaven" (Matt. 6:10). This is where being global comes in. It means nothing more than taking this prayer seriously. It's seeking God's kingdom here on this globe. Common Christianity would be saying that prayer every Sunday in church but never seeking to live it out on this globe.
2. David Bryant, *In the Gap* (Ventura, Calif.: Regal Books, 1985), 93.
3. For more on this, see Dallas Willard, *The Spirit of the Disciplines* (San Francisco: Harper and Row, 1988).
4. Please understand that I am not advocating salvation by works, or righteousness by works, or a righteousness that comes from the Law. Biblically, all one has to do is read Romans or Galatians to see that Paul will not allow these to enter into our theology. But there must be a balance. We cannot say that we can come to faith and salvation in Christ and choose to go on and live *however we please*. You can read several passages in Scripture that contain words of Jesus suggesting that "how we live does matter"; examine Matt. 25:14-46; Luke 6:46-49; and Luke 13:1-9 for starters. Sometimes I think we have been so diligent to guard the truth of "salvation by grace, through faith alone" that we have forgotten that our actions do matter to God. I think the best balance of this in Scripture is the tension between verses 9 and 10 of Eph. 2. Paul ties "by works" and "not by works" together, saying (beginning in verse 8), "For it is by grace you have been saved, through faith—and this not from yourselves, it is the gift of God—*not by works*, so that no one can boast. For we are God's workmanship, created in Christ Jesus *to do good works*" (italics added).
5. Bill and Amy Stearns, *Catch the Vision 2000* (Minneapolis: Bethany House Publishers, 1991), 15.
6. Robertson McQuilkin, *The Great Omission* (Grand Rapids: Baker Book House, 1984), 51-53. For another great story along these same lines, read "Parable of the Orange Trees" in John White's *The Race* (Downers Grove, Ill.: InterVarsity Press, 1984).
7. Charles Edward White, "What Wesley Practiced and Preached About Money" in *Mission Frontiers* 16, No. 9-10 (September-October 1994), 23.
8. Wesley also offered four challenging questions to help people determine how to spend their money when faced with a purchasing opportunity (quoted from White, 24):
    1. In spending this money, am I acting like I own it, or am I acting like the Lord's trustee?
    2. What scripture requires me to spend this money this way?
    3. Can I offer up this purchase as a sacrifice to the Lord?
    4. Will God reward me for this expenditure at the resurrection of the just?

9. James McLeish, ed., *Faithful Witness: The Urbana '84 Compendium* (Downers Grove, Ill.: InterVarsity Press, 1985), 139.

10. Ralph Winter, "Commitment to a Wartime Lifestyle" in *Mission Frontiers,* 20.

11. Paul Borthwick, *A Mind for Missions* (Colorado Springs: NavPress, 1987), 49.

12. Ibid., 44.

13. McQuilkin, *The Great Omission,* 85.

14. Henry T. Blackaby and Claude V. King, *Experiencing God: Knowing and Doing the Will of God* (Nashville: Lifeway Press, 1990), 14, 28.

15. Roberta Winter, "The Non-Essentials of Life," *Mission Frontiers,* 25-26.

16. Ibid.

17. Henri Nouwen et. al., *Compassion* (New York: Doubleday, 1982), 69.

18. Much of the tone and some of the words here were borrowed from George Verwer, as quoted in *Urban Mission,* John E. Kyle, ed. (Downers Grove, Ill.: InterVarsity Press, 1988), 124.